What Is Value Investing?

Lawrence A. Cunningham

McGraw-Hill

New York   Chicago   San Francisco   Lisbon
London   Madrid   Mexico City   Milan
New Delhi   San Juan   Seoul   Singapore
Sydney   Toronto

1 2 3 4 5 6 7 8 9 0   AGM/AGM   0 9 8 7 6 5 4

ISBN 0-07-142955-7

McGraw-Hill books are available at special quantity discounts to use as
premiums and sales promotions, or for use in corporate training programs.
For more information, please write to the Director of Special Sales,
Professional Publishing, McGraw-Hill, Two Penn Plaza, New York, NY
10121-2298. Or contact your local bookstore.

Library of Congress Cataloging-in-Publication Data

Cunningham, Lawrence A., 1962-
      What is value investing? / by Lawrence A. Cunningham.
  p.   cm.
  ISBN 0-07-142955-7 (pbk. : alk. paper)
  1. Investments. 2. Corporations—Valuation. I. Title.

HG4521.C9525 2004
332.63'2042--dc22   2003021901

CONTENTS

CHAPTER 1

TODAY'S INVESTING STYLES

Value investing is fashionable again. During the late 1990s stock mania, a minority of investors habitually sought stocks priced at a discount from value. They avoided the massive losses suffered by most investors who played the market by using a speculation-inspired margin of danger. While the latter group boasted seemingly high short-term gains, value investors came out ahead in the long run. Despite value investing's renaissance, many lack a clear idea of what it is. This short book provides it.

Five investing styles dominate today:

- *Value investors* rely on fundamental analysis of companies' financial performance to identify stocks priced below intrinsic value (the present value of a company's future cash flows, discussed in ensuing chapters). This strategy dates back to Benjamin Graham and David L. Dodd of Columbia University in the 1930s. It has gained favor since the 1970s and 1980s because Berkshire Hathaway Inc. CEO and Chairman Warren E. Buffett has embraced it.

- *Growth investors* seek companies whose earnings gains promise to boost intrinsic value rapidly. Investor and author Philip A. Fisher pioneered this value investing variation in the late 1950s. Magellan Fund manager Peter Lynch boldly extended it in the 1980s.

- *Index investors* buy shares that replicate a large market segment such as the Standard & Poor's 500. Graham endorsed the virtues of this stock selection strategy for defensive investors. Vanguard Fund founder John C. Bogle popularized the method in the 1980s.

- *Technical investors* use charts to glean market behavior indicating whether expectations are rising or falling, market trends, and other "momentum" indicators. This technique is championed by *Investor's Business Daily* founder William J. O'Neil and was widely practiced during the late 1990s.

1

- *Portfolio investors* ascertain their appetite for investment risk and assemble a diversified securities portfolio bearing that risk level. The theory was developed in the 1950s, perfected in the 1970s by a group of Nobel Prize winning economists, and popularized beginning in the early 1970s by Princeton University economist Burton G. Malkiel in his famous book *A Random Wal.k Down Wall Street*.

All investment philosophies center on the perceived relationship between price and value. Value and growth investors think value and price are different; index investors aren't sure they can figure out the relationship; technical investors care only about price, not value; and portfolio investors think price is value.

These beliefs entail different strategies:

- *Value investors* seek stocks of companies priced below value;
- *Growth investors* seek stocks of companies whose near-term growth indicates value, justifying current price;
- *Index investors* think the safest strategy is to buy stocks representing substantially the whole market;
- *Technical investors* seek stocks that can be quickly sold at higher prices; and
- *Portfolio investors* believe that since price and value are identical, price changes measure risk, and investors should pick a mix of securities bearing the desired risk level.

Table 1.1 illustrates the key tenets of the five investing styles.

To illustrate, suppose IBM shares closed yesterday on the New York Stock Exchange at $50 per share. Whether to buy the stock depends on different factors in each investment philosophy. (Whether to sell involves conceptually reciprocal considerations, discussed further in Chapter 8.)

- *Value investors* (a) ask what is the present value of IBM's predicted future cash flows and is it more or less than $50 per share, and (b) buy the stock only if the answer is at least $60. [The $10 difference between value and price indicates a 20-percent "margin of safety" ($10 / $50 = 20 percent); very conservative value investors insist on an even thicker margin.]

Table 1.1. Investing Styles

STYLE	EXEMPLAR	PRICE-VALUE RELATIONSHIP	PRESCRIPTION
Value	Graham/Dodd Buffett	Variable and ascertainable	Focus on value, seek current value greater than current price
Growth	Fisher/Lynch	Variable and ascertainable	Focus on growth, seek value rising faster than price reflects
Index	Bogle	Uncertain and unascertainable	Ignore price-value and buy the "market"
Technical	O'Neil	May be related, but irrelevant	Focus on price trends
Portfolio	Malkiel	Identical	Match risk appetite to price-value risk measurement

- *Growth investors* (a) emphasize the relative probable growth in IBM's sales, earnings, and cash flows, and (b) buy the stock if they believe its value and price will grow towards $60 in the near future.

- *Index investors* (a) throw up their hands when considering price versus value of individual stocks, and (b) simply buy a fund that in turn buys shares of IBM and hundreds of other firms.

- *Technical investors* (a) remain alert for clues rumbling around the marketplace to gauge the likelihood that IBM's price is bound to move above or below $50 imminently, and (b) buy the stock if rumors suggest upward price trends (this group might also engage in short selling if they perceive downward price trends, locking in the $50 price now and committing to buy the stock in the future at a hoped-for lower price).

- *Portfolio investors* (a) say this is all a waste of time because the $50 price of IBM represents the current value of IBM shares, and (b) the important question is whether IBM's risk (measured by its historical stock price volatility compared to the overall market's volatility) suits an investor's risk appetite.

Value and growth investing philosophies overlap. They share the same view of the price-value relationship. But they emphasize different aspects of the future. Value investing emphasizes known values and compares these to price. Growth investing emphasizes expected values arising from growth and compares these to price. In this sense, growth investing is a cousin of value investing. Proponents agree that it is possible for an investment analyst to determine value and then compare it to price.

Index investing is for those unable or unwilling to do so. No special skill or homework is required. Returns will reflect overall index performance rather than that of selected stocks. Devotees of value or growth investing believe this to be the preferred method for those lacking skill or time to conduct proper analysis. (Knowing the basic philosophy of value investing can still help such passive investors understand what is moving their generic investment, a point illustrated in Chapter 12.)

Value investors see technical trading as speculation, not investing. It attempts to anticipate trends in investors' outlooks and to detect patterns in stock price histories from which to extract predictions. It is not much of an investment methodology. Its time frame is also too short to constitute investment. This does not appeal to the rationally inclined analyst and becomes intoxicating during sustained market rallies. The 1990s were the peak of drunkenness.

A species of technical trading, called "momentum trading," was pervasive in the late 1990s. Allure deepened as prices of the most speculative stocks climbed. Practitioners mistakenly believed they were deft stock pickers. Many gloated despite never even considering what a company did, whether it made money, and never looking at a company's financial statements. Self-congratulations were irresistible during a five-year period when prices rose on the vast majority of stocks, even those whose businesses were shaky at best.

During that period, many new investors were drawn to stock markets, though they did not know how to read a financial statement or what fundamentals were. Even seasoned investors succumbed to widespread belief in rumors and impressions rather than analysis of facts and data. Inexperienced investors never heard of value investing and many seasoned participants believed the so-called "new economy" made a fossil of it. History is full of similar periods, the best known being the 1920s, which culminated in the Great Crash of 1929.

It was that economic calamity that led Benjamin Graham and David L. Dodd to synthesize the philosophy of value investing. The investment atmosphere of the late 1920s was characterized by portfolio management techniques driven by inside information and impressions. Graham helped to improve investor discipline by articulating an intellectual framework for investing philosophy. His value investing blueprint is judgment-laden but gives investors a sturdy foundation.

Portfolio investing is a more ambitious attempt to provide an intellectual framework for investment philosophy. Its key hypothesis is that price equals value. If this so-called "efficient market hypothesis" were true, there would be no place for value investing. It would not be possible to achieve superior investment results by buying stocks whose prices are safely below intrinsic business values (the present value of future cash flows).

In efficient markets, a company's business risks are reflected in the historical variation of its stock price relative to that of other companies. This key portfolio investing metric is routinely measured by its devotees and known as a stock's *beta*. Advisors use this *beta* risk measure to steer portfolio investors into investments that best match their risk appetites. (Chapter 7 gives additional details.)

Portfolio theory takes one further big step. It says that it is possible, by assembling a diversified basket of securities, to eliminate all the specific risks accompanying any single one. The risks of one are offset by the rewards of the remainder. Portfolio investing boils down to analyzing *beta* and designing an optimally diverse portfolio. Volumes of elaborate mathematical and econometric studies have researched these tools. Some evidence supports the theory, and other evidence casts doubt.

Value investors are skeptics of efficiency theory, its proposition that price and value are identical, and the idea that *beta* is a useful measure of risk. Their investment records contribute to a significant body of empirical evidence that suggests weaknesses in the theory. There are too many successful value investors for efficiency backers to ignore. Too many stocks appear to be priced at above or below value for the efficiency story to be complete. And while *beta* may measure some risks of price fluctuations, it is not a mirror of business performance or value.

Market bubbles are not accidents, but symptoms of a business environment typically characterized by rapid technological innovation and disproportionate excitement. Exuberance spirals, spreading farther and wider than its audience comprehends. Droves of ordinary people begin falsely to think they understand businesses and stock markets. Experienced investors pursue businesses beyond their competence to understand.

Market depressions are not accidents either, but symptoms of opposite forces—novices withdraw and experts show disproportionate fear. Hangovers disproportionately feel worse and last longer than the joy and duration of the party prelude.

Value investors don't believe stock markets can be predicted, over short or long periods. What can be ascertained, with a modest degree of reliability, is the probable performance of underlying businesses over long periods, based on past performance and current information. Value investors analyze this information to ascertain value and relate this to price.

C H A P T E R   2

VALUE INVESTING TRADITIONS

Value investing is partly a state of mind. It is characterized by habitually relating the price of a stock to the value of the underlying business. Basic principles of fundamental analysis are the tools. They arise from three traditions.

Benjamin Graham's margin of safety principle is the first one. It requires assurance that a stock's price is substantially below its estimated value. The test requires conducting a full business analysis. To begin, value investors use simple filters that narrow the range of candidates to those that an investor understands and can evaluate (commonly known as a circle of competence).

John Burr Williams refined value investing's second core tradition. This quantitative tradition requires estimating a company's intrinsic value measured by the present value of its probable future cash flows, conservatively estimated using current data. This principle captures the intuition that a dollar in hand today is worth more than a dollar paid in the future. (Chapters 5, 6, and 7 provide details.)

Philip A. Fisher added value investing's third tradition. This qualitative tradition requires the diligent investor to find a company exhibiting strong long-term prospects. These are indicated by characteristics creating a business franchise, such as consumer loyalty, unmatched brand-name recognition, and formidable market power. Also relevant are high-quality managers who can be counted on to channel the franchise's rewards to the company's shareholders.

Warren E. Buffett is the consummate and best-known integrator of these three traditions. Buffett practices a comprehensive method of value investing. He refers to the exercise simply as investing, viewing the modifier "value" as redundant. Other disciples weight the components differently, producing a range of value investing styles. All are united by appreciating the difference between price and value.

GRAHAM: THE FATHER OF VALUE INVESTING

Benjamin Graham's *The Intelligent Investor* is the classic work on value investing by the philosophy's chief architect and greatest exponent. Many have read the book, originally published in 1949 and in several subsequent editions. The key idea is to protect against error by developing a long-term strategy and stock selection framework.

Graham's more detailed *Security Analysis*, coauthored with David L. Dodd, elaborates the deeper architecture (devotees regard the second edition, published in 1940, as the most informative version). Emphasis is on the balance sheet (assets and liabilities) to determine business value. Current editions of that classic, written by others, also stress analyzing the income statement (revenues and expenses) to appraise value.

Debate centers on whether these texts are timeless classics or outdated. Neither extreme position is correct; in fact, they are both partly right. Critics complain that the original editions are outdated because they emphasize businesses of the day such as railroads, utilities, and heavy manufacturing, and Graham focused on the balance sheet and asset values; today's businesses depend on greater contribution from nonphysical assets, and the investment community focuses more heavily on the cash that assets generate rather than the values assigned to them on balance sheets.

True, the prose of *Security Analysis* and *The Intelligent Investor* is somewhat old-fashioned and comparatively dense. Graham's contemporaries were primarily professionals willing to wade through heavy reading. Today's investors are more diverse, drawn from numerous vocations, and accustomed to breezier writing. Our era's information intensity and shorter attention spans demand briefer trots.

Today's economic environment encompasses more varied businesses ranging from on-line music to pharmaceuticals, enlarging the domain beyond Graham's favored business illustrations. Contemporary businesses use a wider variety of asset classes and varying degrees of reliance on hard assets versus intangible assets. Values in copyrights and patents often surpass those of traditional industrial assets.

Still, Graham's key principles endure. The bedrock principle remains the "margin of safety"—paying a price far enough below value to avoid major capital market losses. The main objective is to preserve capital. Paying too much risks the excess to marketplace hazards and the vagaries of a company's business. This principle is akin to the overriding tenet of medicine, first do no harm (*primum non nocere*)—first, lose no money.

Graham defined investments as economic positions which, upon analysis, promise safety of principal and an adequate return (at least equal to the rate of inflation). Anything else is speculation, he thought. The philosophy opposes speculation, in favor of good businesses for the long term. It requires evaluating companies, whether Anheuser-Busch, Microsoft, or Zeneca. The principles generally do not work over short time horizons but can be very rewarding over generations.

Graham furnished a 10-point analytical screen for investment selection. Half-measured financial strength and half-measured risk aspects. Critical on the financial strength side were a high ratio of current assets to current liabilities and sparing use of long-term debt compared to book value and liquidation value. (Chapter 4 explains these metrics.) To reduce risk, Graham limited prudent selections to firms with returns measured by earnings at least twice that of high-grade corporate bonds and whose current price-to-earnings level is less than half the highest such level over the past five years. (Chapter 6 discusses these points.)

Graham knew that luck, good and bad, plays a role in investing (and life), but that luck does not control everything. The goal is to limit Lady Luck's downside. Contemporary violators are day trading, momentum tactics, and market timing. All are high-risk practices intended to exploit market movements using nonvalue criteria. Current strategies embracing the traditional philosophy include slowly, carefully building a collection of a manageable number of understandable investments, as well as dollar-cost averaging (the practice of investing set dollar amounts in a particular security at designated intervals, discussed further in Chapter 12).

Graham divided the investor universe into two broad categories: defensive and enterprising. For either, however, minimizing losses is more important than maximizing gains. With losses minimized, average gains generate above-average results.

FISHER: PIONEER OF GROWTH EMPHASIS

Graham focused on financial analysis of companies, paying less attention to management quality or business environment. Fisher enlarged fundamental analysis by focusing on these qualitative aspects.

Management is important to growth companies, and assumes greater importance for all companies amid accelerated business change and given innovation in risk management and business strategy.

Fisher appreciated such business tactics as brand-name development and product packaging that create value, economic goodwill, and the ability to generate returns on equity greater than industry or peer averages. That power can be leveraged in a globalizing world where brand name can be established worldwide and used as a launching pad for additional product lines or extensions. Examples include entertainment companies marketing multilingual versions of a product in print, cinematic, VHS, DVD, and Web formats.

Fisher narrowed the number of value investment candidates by emphasizing that even companies priced below intrinsic value could be lousy investments. Businesses can be underpriced for valid reasons, such as poor management. Attractively priced investments also turn mediocre when they become fully priced, in his view.

In Fisher's era, investment wealth arose either from traditional value investing (buying underpriced securities and holding them until fairly priced or overpriced) or fairly-priced businesses poised to grow so rapidly in sales and earnings (today we would add cash flows) that profits arise from that growth. The former describes traditional Graham-based pure value investing. The latter is Fisher's pioneering sense as a growth rather than a value investor and leads to the distinction (somewhat false) between the two.

Fisher furnished a 15-point checklist to identify a growth company. It includes whether the company's potential markets are large enough to enable many years of sales growth. Consider the difference in reaching a market-saturation point between automobile manufacturers and makers of car batteries. Amid globalization, market expansion is greater for global companies able to distribute existing products worldwide and respond with new products ideally tailored to regional tastes.

WILLIAMS: CASH FLOW'S ROLE

The value of a business, a share of stock, or any other productive asset is the present value of its future cash flows. Williams elaborated this point, emphasizing what developed into discounted cash flow (DCF) analysis, today's most popular valuation methodology. Its popularity, however, hides the important reality that value is easier to define than to measure (easier said than done). The tools Graham and Fisher developed remain crucial in this exercise.

One hazard of undue reliance on DCF analysis is a temptation to classify stocks as either value stocks or growth stocks. Many professionals, including those at mutual funds, try to differentiate their products from others using this distinction. But it is a distinction with limited difference.

Valuing a business (or any productive asset) requires estimating its probable future performance and discounting the results to present value. The probable future performance includes whatever growth (or shrinkage) is assumed.

So growth (or lack of it) is integral to a valuation exercise. This supports the point that the phrase value investing is redundant: Investing is the deliberate determination that one pays a price lower than the value being obtained. Only speculators pay a price hoping that through growth the value rises above it.

Despite this nomenclature confusion, value investing is conventionally defined as buying companies bearing low ratios of price-to-earnings, price-to-book value, or high dividend yields. But these metrics do not by themselves make a company a value investment. It isn't that simple. Nor does the absence of such metrics prevent an investment from bearing a sufficient margin of safety and qualitative virtues to justify its inclusion in a value investor's portfolio.

Growth doesn't equate directly with value either. Growing earnings can mean growing value. But growing earnings can also mean growing expenses, and sometimes expenses growing faster than revenues. Growth adds value only when the payoff from growth is greater than the cost of growth. A company reinvesting a dollar of earnings to grow by 99 cents is not helping its shareholders and is not a value stock, though it may be a growth stock.

BUFFET: INTEGRATOR

Warren Buffett brings these points together. Value investing consists of analyzing businesses within one's circle of competence to find those whose return on incremental capital is high, compared to what capital costs, and then investing in those that can be bought most cheaply. Table 2.1 summarizes value investing's key figures and their major contributions.

Table 2.1 Value Investing's Architects

FIGURE	ROLE	KEY POINTS	WRITINGS
Graham	Father of value of investing	Margin of safety; focus on balance sheet; 10-point checklist	*The Intelligent Investor; Security Analysis; The Interpretation of Financial Statements*
Fisher	Qualitative dimension, growth role	Scuttlebutt; focus on earnings; 15-point checklist	*Common Stocks and Uncommon Profits*
Williams	Discounted cash flow analysis	Focus on cash	*The Theory of Investment Value*
Buffett	Integration	Circle of competence; business analysis	*The Essays of Warren Buffett: Lessons for Corporate America* (compilation of annual letters)

VARIATIONS ON THE THEME

There are many variations on the value investing theme. The philosophy permits particular applications that vary to suit individual taste and ability. Leading value investors employ a range of styles.

Fisher is a good example. Many contrast Graham, the father of value investing, and Fisher, the father of growth investing. But because value investing and growth investing are really cousins of one another, Fisher is better understood as developing a variation on value investing's themes. The difference is more a matter of style and emphasis than fundamentals.

Among the most famous published accounts of success reported by students of Graham-Dodd's teachings is Buffett's essay *The Superinvestors of Graham-and-Doddsville*. He documents a range of value investors who adopted varying styles of the philosophy. Some diversify investments widely while others allocate wealth to a concentrated group of stocks. Most place a high premium on understanding the particulars of any business before investing, yet some will invest while holding only a reasonable level of expertise on a business.

Columbia University Business School professor Bruce Greenwald published a series of essays updating and elaborating Buffett's *Superinvestors* theme. He highlights numerous value investors to underscore slight variations of approach. Some refine valuation methods to define value as what informed industrialists would pay to own a business's equivalent assets. Some relate historical price fluctuations to intrinsic business value. Others combine this innovation with more traditional valuation metrics to enhance investment discipline. Some emphasize the role of catalysts such as takeovers and bankruptcy reorganizations that can transform underpriced businesses into realized investment results.

Of the variety of value investors and their styles, those most closely aligned to Graham might be called pure value investors. Those giving more weight to other traditions or contemporary influences might loosely be described as modified value investors. However described, the fusing theme among value investors is appreciating the difference between stock price and business value. All also believe in the gospel of the margin of safety. A common characteristic is superior investment results.

THE REST OF US

Value investing is challenging. Ascertaining business quality and estimating value are difficult. Many curious investors who learn what value investing requires opt for the busy person's version of contemporary intelligent investing: the index fund. As index investing's leading exponent John C. Bogle has quipped, value investing is the second most promising investing philosophy. For those lacking requisite discipline to conduct value investing, Bogle's quip is apt. For those possessing knowledge of value investing, there is no better method.

Compare the returns on two of America's most prominent investment options in the past few decades: the Magellan Fund, made famous by Peter Lynch's growth variation on value investing, and the S&P 500, represnting Bogle's famous index approach to investing. Between 1971 and 2000, Magellan outperformed the S&P index in the most years, usually by significant margins. In the handful of years when the S&P index outperformed Magellan, it generally did so modestly. Table 2.2 shows the comparison.

Requisite intelligence for value investing is moderate, not requiring Mensa-level genius. However, it requires common sense and good judgment. Exercising those faculties, in turn, depends on a refined intellectual framework that helps an investor resist emotional temptations. Practitioners should adapt and incorporate the framework to meet their particular needs.

Value investing partakes of a certain intellectual curiosity. Devotees tend to be interested in ideas. They read books on business analysis and investing, an important exercise considering that no single book (this one included) can furnish everything required on any given subject (investing included).

Some high-profile value investors are also inclined to write about their craft. Graham, Fisher, and Williams all wrote books explaining their trade. Others emulate Buffett's practice of writing letters to investors elaborating their philosophies.

Reading and rereading quality investment books and essays expands one's perspective. In addition to the writings of the investors and authors mentioned above (and this book's author), reliable treatments of value investing include the books written by Robert G. Hagstrom, Janet C. Lowe, Timothy P. Vick, and Martin J. Whitman.

As experience enriches a reader's investment knowledge, it becomes increasingly clear that value investing is a foundation philosophy. Studying its principles through a cool, calculating, logical method produces an outlook and frame of mind that's more of a philosophy than a toolbox. Tools are important—and this book mentions the key ones—but an intellectual foundation remains the distinguishing hallmark.

Table 2.2 Value versus Indexing

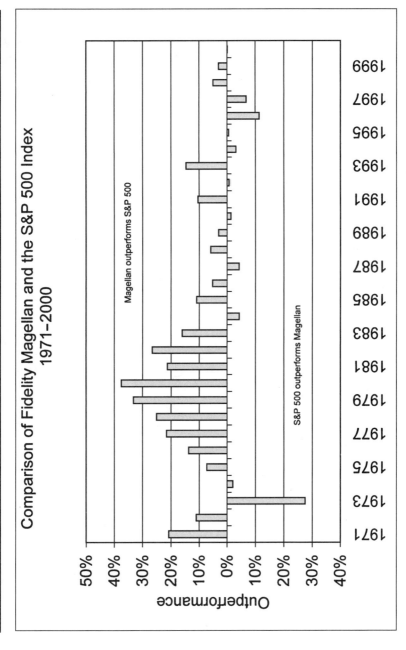

Comparison of Fidelity Magellan and the S&P 500 Index
1971–2000

Source: Meir Statman & Jonathan Scheid, *Buffett in Foresight and Hindsight* (Santa Clara University Working Paper No. 00/01-37, June 2001)

Value investors are open-minded. They are not technicians and do not practice a how-to shop. They know how to select the right tool for the job. This knowledge requires a sense of history, business, accounting, good judgment, basic human psychology, and specific knowledge necessary to understand particular businesses (actuarial science for insurance, consumer preferences for fashion goods, informational appetites for media companies).

CHAPTER 3

CIRCLES OF COMPETENCE

Value investing involves business analysis. It requires grasping a company's operating environment, and the only way to do this successfully is to focus on companies the investor can reasonably understand. The universe of companies within an investor's intellectual grasp is called his or her circle of competence. Elementary principles of value investing are to define clearly one's circle of competence and stay within its boundaries.

BUSINESSES

Value investors determine whether they understand a business by assessing their familiarity with its products, customers, and operating climate. An investor's interests and tastes influence competencies, and one's own industry is a good starting point. An individual's consumer habits are another. Locally-based companies are a third.

Value investors quiz themselves. They ask: What products does the company sell or what services does it provide? How are they used? Do customers need these things? How stable is demand, and how well positioned is the company to meet it going forward? How distinctive is the company's product compared to possible substitutes? Do consumers care, and how much? How likely is it that this company can raise prices without losing sales (called franchise value or economic goodwill, and discussed in Chapter 6)?

Who is the company's target customer/client base? Does the company depend on one or a few customers for most of its revenues, or does it have millions of customers? How much does any dependency matter—how financially solid is a major customer?

How does the company sell its products? What is the company's geographic market? How sensitive is it to economic downturns in that market?

Can the company adapt quickly to changing economic and business conditions? How strong is the company's supply chain? Its employee relations? Does it operate in regions subject to ordinary or extraordinary political or economic risks? Is the company a classic, vintage, or rookie?

Value investors look at relevant business patterns: products and their degree of brand or commodity characteristics; the sources and costs of supply; the distribution chain; customer habits and tastes; and business organization and design. They question how a business has handled factors such as globalization, the rise of the Internet and e-commerce, the move toward service-based profit centers with fewer physical assets.

Assessing these basics solves two problems: It determines whether a business is within an investor's circle of competence and begins the process of determining whether it is a suitable investment candidate. For investors who cannot ascertain this information intelligently, the company is outside their circle of competence. If they can do so, they think about how these factors impact the company's ability to generate future profit.

Answering these questions requires information. Public disclosure and news reports generate substantial information that investors use to assemble corporate profiles. Fisher famously approached the information-assessment challenge using what he called the "scuttlebutt" method—talking to everyone knowledgeable about a company, from suppliers to workers to customers and other industry participants and experts.

Professional investors have the time and influence to do this. Most nonprofessionals must rely on public information, whose volume seems to multiply annually. While devotees of efficient market theory deny that this information is useful to investors when selecting investments, value investors consider it essential to conducting business analysis.

Superior results are a function of a company's franchise characteristics in a competitive environment. Franchise characteristics enable a company to generate comparatively high returns on equity—that is earnings on shareholder investment greater than what it costs to raise incremental capital. The franchise sustains these when it neutralizes the threat of drawing competitors to dissipate those returns.

Examples are legal barriers such as patents or government licenses. Less visible are consumer franchises fastened by brand loyalty, as with products including Coke or Harley Davidson. Some value investors believe that such franchise characteristics are the key reasons a business may be able to generate sustained periods of high returns on equity and beneficial earnings growth.

Insights gained from assessing a company's competitive position form crucial judgments in any valuation analysis. Relevant inputs in this exercise include factors such as profit margins and capital costs. Into those factors go assessments of industry economics, company advantages or disadvantages, and related sustainability.

Most of these factors will be captured in the reported financial results that constitute the valuation framework, discussed in later chapters. To reach these judgments and use these tools, however, value investors must feel confident that the target investment is within their circle of competence.

A related component of the circle of competence concerns managerial qualities. Our era's shorthand buzzword for this value investing focus is corporate governance. This is important because it establishes the means by which corporate results are channeled to shareholders or others. Commentators discuss components such as adopting best practices, fixing an ideal board size, and establishing the right board committees.

Important as these are, managers are the most important element of corporate governance. Value investors seek companies run by able and honest managers. Shareholders of the most wonderful businesses can be damaged by poor managers. Using all information available, value investors seek managers indicating they march to the investor's beat. So in addition to questions about business fundamentals, value investors ask tough questions concerning who manages a company and whether they are both capable and trustworthy. Inability to make such determinations likewise puts an investment candidate beyond an investor's circle of competence.

ACCOUNTING'S PART IN CIRCLES OF COMPETENCE

Accounting is crucial to value investing, making a basic grasp of it relevant to the circle of competence. It is the hinge of capital allocation, with properly applied accounting putting capital in the best hands and misleading or misunderstood accounting squandering it. Value investors understand accounting as a way to present information, not an end in itself. Nonvalue investors don't always appreciate this.

Take a classic illustrative case. It concerned a dividend decision facing a corporate board of directors. The company held stock in another company with a tax basis of $30 million and a current market price of $4 million, and its board decided to withdraw from the investment. Consider two alternatives to do so.

Plan A would distribute the stock as a dividend. That would reduce the asset and owners' equity columns of the balance sheet. Stockholders would get $4 million. Plan B would sell the stock, take a hit to income of $26 million for accounting and income tax purposes, and thus reduce tax liability by about $8 million. The company would then distribute the $4 million proceeds it would have distributed under plan A, plus the $8 million tax savings as a distribution to shareholders.

The board chose Plan A, though Plan B looks more economically rational. It did so because it judged that many market participants pay more attention to income than to asset levels and wanted to avoid having the market punish its stock price. Under attack by shareholders, a judge permitted the director decision to stand, deferring to the board's judgment. The market does often respond more to cosmetics than to fundamentals.

This market appetite can produce in corporate cultures greater interest in finessing the figures (wagging the dog by the tail) than making sound business decisions. Enron Corp. is an example. It attached greater importance to superior accounting (maximizing reported accounting income) than superior economics (maximizing after-tax cash available to shareholders). Enron's risk management policy expressly adopted this stance, favoring "accounting rather than economic performance." The policy stated:

> Reported earnings follow the rules and principles of accounting. The results do not always create measures consistent with underlying economics. However, corporate management's performance is generally measured by accounting income, not underlying economics. Risk management strategies are therefore directed at accounting rather than economic performance.

This gets the world backwards, destroying the sense that accounting is a tool, not an end. It is a device to record reality and a vehicle to assess it. It is not reality itself. The representation it creates is like a painting, possible to create and analyze from multiple perspectives. But just as artists and critics develop a body of canonical tests of composition and craft, accounting's reduction of complex reality to tabulated simplicity is governed by rules of judgment and faith. So accounting knowledge is part of a value investor's circle of competence, along with knowledge of business and governance. See Figure 3.1.

The old joke tells of the manager who asks his accountant "How much is 2 + 2?," and the accountant replies, "How much would you like it to be?" It is less useful to know that the manager and accountant say the result of their mathematical gymnastics is 3, 4, or 5, than it is to know what rules they applied in coming up with their answer.

Though more complex, problems like these arise when financial issues are implicated. Examples include when to recognize a sale as complete, how much to reserve for the likelihood that some customers will not pay their bills for merchandise shipped, and how financial hedging transactions should be measured. These decisions can cut for investors or against them, and value investors know how they tend to

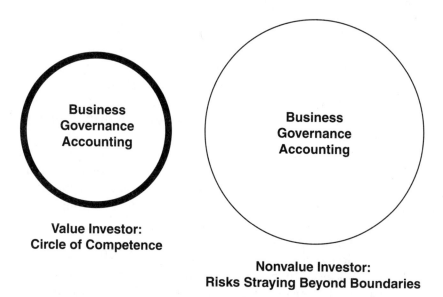

**Business
Governance
Accounting**

**Business
Governance
Accounting**

**Value Investor:
Circle of Competence**

**Nonvalue Investor:
Risks Straying Beyond Boundaries**

Value investors limit their selections to those of businesses they understand, with governance structures and managerial qualities they can comfortably assess, and for which they understand the basic accounting. The resulting universe may be relatively small compared to the universe nonvalue investors trade in. But the boundaries are clearly underscored. In other words, the size of one's circle is not that important, but knowing its boundaries is essential.

Figure 3.1. Knowing one's limits.

be cut at companies they consider investing in. (Chapters 9 through 11 give more examples.)

This is what it means to know a little accounting. Certified public accountants (CPAs) know accounting in the ultimate sense, as masters. Investors who share that knowledge might have an advantage in that aspect of investing. But it is not essential. Value investors possess a modicum of accounting knowledge and insight, even if they are not masters of it.

What this requires is a familiarity with the basic landscape—financial statements and their relationships to each other, the major categories of accounts that appear in these statements, the sources of accounting authority, and the range of discretion and judgment that accounting rules allow and require (and the temptations this creates for managers to massage the numbers). This is generally taught in a fundamental accounting course.

While accounting addresses recording, measuring, and aggregating data, its most profound challenge is making judgments concerning how and when to classify financial transactions. At each stage, choices are presented. For resulting reports to have meaning for investors, accountants try to establish "answers" for how to treat various events.

That way, all the numerical data, perhaps even including some bottom-line numbers, are a reliable basis for understanding how well or poorly a company is doing compared to prior periods or to rivals. This is achieved by promulgating and using unified principles designed to address the infinite variety of transactions that accounting must grapple with.

Those principles are embodied in a set of accounting guidelines called generally accepted accounting principles (GAAP). Many sources contribute to GAAP. The main principles are the product of agreement among the accounting profession's leaders, a group called the Financial Accounting Standards Board (FASB).

Many accounting pronouncements result from years of disagreement, negotiation, controversy, and compromise. GAAP are the result of choices FASB makes. Choices are not the product of any scientific process that can be verified. GAAP are best understood as conventions; their purpose is to facilitate the comparability of financial statements among business and over time.

In reality, there can be more than one "right" way to account for a certain kind of financial event. In many such cases, FASB has elected to permit alternatives to handle the matter, but only so long as the chosen way is accepted under GAAP and fully disclosed as part of the financial statements.

Accounting standard setters are guided by a series of objectives that financial accounting and reporting seek to meet. These include such basic ideas as providing useful information to outsiders, particularly investors, including information relating to assets, liabilities, and equity and changes in them over time.

What results is an elaborate system that attempts to simplify complex decisions by boiling down enormous numbers and types of transactions into a single set of financial reports. GAAP often has positions at odds with intuition. Yet they have their own logic, rooted in these fundamental ideas and basic principles. Value investors have some familiarity with these heuristics.

Accounting complexity increases with business complexity. Value investors limit their investment selections to businesses they understand and for which the accounting is likewise within their competence to assess. They also appreciate accounting process characteristics. It is neither necessary nor possible to catalogue the full range of challenges accounting faces in distilling economic reality into usable financial reports. Examples in later chapters give a useful flavor.

CHAPTER 4

FINANCIAL ANALYSIS

The balance sheet is a record of historical facts that allows users to help gauge the future; the income statement is a picture of past performance, which is more likely to vary. It is a mistake to ignore either. In fact, the single most important measure of historical business performance is return on equity, measured as earnings divided by book value—an income statement item divided by a balance sheet entry. It is important because it measures the results obtained for shareholders on their invested capital.

Because ultimate value resides in future cash flows, a third accounting statement is also crucial: the statement of cash flows. The cash flow statement's chief virtue is it reverses discretionary exercises that enter into preparing the income statement and balance sheet. Together, the three statements, when properly prepared and accompanied by narrative explanation, give a complete picture of a company's business and financial condition.

Graham favored using the balance sheet as the principal aid to business analysis, supplemented by the income statement. Both remain crucial. Since Graham's time, however, the cash flow statement became fully developed and now serves as a useful supplemental source of information.

Value investing requires examining a company's business and financial condition. Calculating and interpreting financial ratios helps do this. They focus on gauging a company's financial strength and risks.

Starting with the balance sheet, is the company able to meet its debts as they come due and how well is it managing its short-term assets and liabilities? Answers are suggested by the *current ratio* and the *quick ratio*.

The current ratio is the relationship between current assets (cash and resources expected to become cash within one year, such as inventory and accounts receivable) and current liabilities (obligations due within one year, such as short-term notes). See Figure 4.1. Graham was a current-ratio hardliner, insisting on a ratio of at least 2-to-1 as a measure of financial strength.

$$\frac{\text{Current Assets}}{\text{Current Liabilities}}$$

Figure 4.1. Current ratio.

Most value investors today recognize that optimal levels vary with business type, and that for most businesses a current ratio between 1 and 2 is ideal. A current ratio below 1 signals liquidity problems; a ratio above 2 signals inefficiency problems—inventory should be moving more quickly or accounts receivables collected more rapidly, or cash reinvested or distributed.

The quick ratio eliminates less liquid current assets from the calculation, focusing more intensely on liquidity—the capacity to meet immediately forthcoming obligations. See Figure 4.2.

The *debt-to-equity ratio* assesses capital structure. It measures a company's leverage—how many dollars of fixed long-term claims exist compared to the residual claims of stockholders. See Figure 4.3. Leverage is valuable, but only up to a point. So a debt-to-equity ratio of 2 or 3 is desirable. But one of 8, 9, or 10 is dangerous, especially if the business can't readily generate sufficient cash to make periodic fixed payments on its debt. Optimal levels vary with relative asset intensity. Again, Graham took a hard line, screening out companies bearing debt-to-equity levels considered modest by contemporary standards.

To test capital structure optimality, value investors consider also the company's *coverage ratio*. This compares net income to interest obligations on debt. See Figure 4.4. Coverage should be several multiples of obligations.

Fisher emphasized qualitative matters such as managerial effectiveness, and some indirect quantitative proxies help the assessment. Tests include the rate of inventory and receivables turnover, as well as the size of profit margins.

Inventory turnover is determined by comparing the relationship between the cost of inventory sold during a period (formally, the cost of goods sold) and the average amount of inventory on hand during the period. See Figure 4.5. High-velocity inventory is a mark of managerial efficiency. Inventory is a cost; idle inventory increases it while speedy inventory turnover reduces it.

Inventory turns vary with business type as well, with dairy farmers turning it far more rapidly than aircraft manufacturers. The issue is how one business compares to its industry peers.

$$\frac{\text{Cash} + \text{Accounts Receivable}}{\text{Current Liabilities}}$$

Figure 4.2. Quick ratio

$$\frac{\text{Total Debt}}{\text{Equity}}$$

Figure 4.3. Debt-to-equity ratio.

$$\frac{\text{Net Income}}{\text{Interest Expense}}$$

Figure 4.4. Coverage ratio

$$\frac{\text{Cost of Goods Sold}}{\text{Average Inventory}}$$

Figure 4.5. Inventory turnover ratio.

$$\frac{\text{Sales on Credit}}{\text{Average Receivables}}$$

Figure 4.6. Receivables turnover ratio.

Rapid receivables collection is a sign of good management too. Letting customers string out debts translates into funding one's customers—an unreimbursed cost to the business. Measuring receivables turns is done by dividing credit sales during a period by the average receivables outstanding during the period. See Figure 4.6.

The speed of turnover is determined by dividing this figure by 365, showing the average number of days receivables are outstanding during a year. Comparing this figure to the company's credit terms and to its peers reveals managerial skill.

Key to business efficiency is the profit per dollar of sales, called the *profit margin.* To calculate it, divide operating income by the total net sales (i.e., sales after returns, discounts, and so on) and express the result as a percentage. (Two alternatives to this standard profit margin calculation are also often used–a more general one called *gross profit margin* divides *gross* profit on sales by total net sales, and a more specific one called *net profit margin* divides *net* income by total net sales.)

There is tremendous variation in profit margins across industries. Average profit margins in the automotive and banking industries, for example, are way lower (often less than 10 percent) than in the computer, pharmaceutical, and food industries (as high as 40 percent in the case of Microsoft).

Profit margins indicate whether a company possesses franchise characteristics. Higher margins mean a company can raise prices without hurting sales. That pricing power indicates a franchise quality. Barriers that protect it can include superior distribution systems, brand name recognition, uniqueness of product, and other value attributes.

Returns are the crucial upshot for value investing: what earnings have been generated from the equity, assets, and investment put at management's disposal? The most important of these—and one of the most important value investing metrics—is the return on equity. As later chapters show, this measurement reveals important clues concerning whether a business possesses franchise value and whether business growth enhances value.

Return on equity is the amount the business earned on the capital owned by its shareholders. Shareholder capital is equal to the total assets minus the total liabilities. See Figure 4.7. If a business earns $10 million on shareholder equity of $100 million, then its return on equity is 10 percent.

Return on investment is the amount a business earned on both the capital owned by its shareholders and the capital supplied by lenders on a long-term (over one year) basis. See Figure 4.8. A business might borrow money rather than issue equity if management believes the firm will generate greater return on the capital than what it costs to borrow it.

$$\frac{\text{Net Income}}{\text{Average Equity}}$$

Figure 4.7. Return on equity (ROE).

$$\frac{\text{Net Income}}{\text{Average Equity + Long-Term Debt}}$$

Figure 4.8. Return on investment (ROI).

Suppose a business with $100 million in shareholder equity borrows $50 million from long-term lenders and then generates earnings of $15 million on that total capital. Its return on investment would be 10 percent (15/150). But this leveraging boosts the business's return on equity—earnings of $15 million on shareholder equity of $100 million means a return on equity of 15 percent.

Using debt to boost return on equity is common but by no means imperative. Some companies generate sufficient cash from operations to enable high returns on equity more cheaply than they could by borrowing. These are particularly attractive to value investors because they suggest franchise characteristics and relatively low business risk.

Return on assets is the amount a business earned on all its resources—not only shareholder equity and long-term borrowing, but also short-term resources generated by effective management of working capital. See Figure 4.9. A business might seek short-term, low-rate loans or buy goods on credit that it resells for cash, thus increasing assets available for deployment at low or no cost. Those assets contribute to incremental increases in earnings, boosting both return on equity and return on investment.

Suppose a business maintains $20 million on average of short-term assets during a year (by continually repaying the obligations as they come due and incurring new ones as rollovers). That could increase incremental annual earnings by say $2 million. So a company with shareholder equity of $100 million, long-term debt of $50 million, carrying that additional $20 million short-term, and earning $17 million generates a return on assets of 10 percent (17/170). This deployment boosts return on investment to 11.3 percent (17/150) and return on equity to 17 percent (17/100).

Return on assets is thus the toughest measure of performance based on returns because it reflects results of deploying all resources at management's disposal. Starting with a high return on assets should yield a high return on investment and hence on equity.

$$\frac{\text{Net Income}}{\text{Average Assets}}$$

Figure 4.9. Return on assets (ROA).

(Some analysts calculate a "financial leverage index" equal to the return on equity divided by the return on assets.) Higher returns on assets are achieved by squeezing earnings out of fewer or smaller asset bases.

Some value investors use a complex formula for measuring return on equity. One approach computes it as the product of profits, production, and capital structure. It multiplies (a) profits as a percentage of sales by (b) sales as a percentage of assets by (c) assets as a percentage of equity. The reason for the elaborate formula is to illustrate the drivers of return on equity: Better profit margins drive higher returns on assets, and higher returns on assets drive higher returns on equity. These drivers are therefore worth direct examination.

Completing the picture of a company's financial performance involves comparing income statement and cash flow data. A useful example is the *quality of income*. It measures cash flows provided by operating activities divided by operating income. It shows what portion of income turned into cash.

An equally useful link compares annual *depreciation expense* with capital expenditures. Depreciation expense is an accounting concept designed to match the original cost of a fixed asset with its future revenue-generating capability. The result is a noncash expense. Some analysts make the mistake of assuming that such expenses can be ignored. But depreciation expense is a useful proxy to gauge future capital investment requirements that will absorb cash. So a complete picture of a business's condition requires relating depreciation expense to future capital needs. (More on this in Chapter 6.)

Value investors evaluate financial statements covering a period of multiple years. Graham favored a look back of a decade or more for many analyses. At a minimum, five years of history is advisable. The examination should consider how various metrics have changed during that significant period of time. This reveals more accurately the company's long-term strengths and weaknesses.

Over short periods, economic fickleness and managerial ingenuity can produce accounting data that obscures longer-term realities. There is no assurance that last year's performance will repeat, nor that of any prior period will, but the farther back the history reaches, the more reliable the data are to gauge future prospects.

CHAPTER 5

COMPOUNDING PRINCIPLES

Value investors appreciate the power of compounding to generate high returns over long periods. Table 5.1 illustrates the basics
(figures are rounded for dramatization). It depicts the future value of
$1000 using various return assumptions and horizons.

The time period alone bears emphasis. At any given rate of
return, sums multiply geometrically over time. Look at the first row,
showing 5 percent. It shows the growth of $1000 into $7000 during
a 40-year period, approximately an investment lifetime. This is not
trivial. The sum nearly doubles over 10 years and nearly triples over
20.

Differing rates of return likewise warrant separate emphasis. For
any given period, sums multiply geometrically at higher returns. For
1 year, rates drive substantial differences by definition, a 25-percent
return being five times greater than a 5-percent return ($1250 com-
pared to $1050). Looking down the column showing a 10-year hori-
zon, the difference between 5 percent and 25 percent is nearly sixfold
($1600 compared to $9300).

Putting time horizons and rates together produces staggering differences. In an investment lifetime—say 40 years—the difference
between annual returns of 5 percent and 25 percent is breathtaking:
$7.5 million compared to $7000. For 15 percent, the sum of $1000
grows into more than a quarter-million dollars in a lifetime
($268,000), a small fortune. Even over 10 years, the sum returning 10
percent nearly triples (to $2600).

Combining horizons and rates of return also reveals the speed of
compounding. A sum more than doubles in 10 years at 10 percent and
more than doubles in 5 years at 20 percent. Table 5.1 shows that a sum
doubles in 5 years at 15 percent. (Due to rounding done in the table,
the figure is actually a little more than double.)

Table 5.1 Compounding: Higher Returns for Longer Terms

The Future Value of $1,000
(compounded annually; more frequent compounding drives higher future values)

	1 YR.	5 YRS.	10 YRS.	20 YRS.	40 YRS.
5%	$1,050	$1,275	$1,600	$2,650	$7,000
10%	$1,100	$1,600	$2,600	$6,700	$45,000
15%	$1,150	$2,000	$4,050	$16,400	$268,000
20%	$1,200	$2,500	$6,200	$38,300	$1.5 million
25%	$1,250	$3,050	$9,300	$86,700	$7.5 million

A rule of thumb emerges: A sum of money doubles when the product of the return and the horizon equals about 72. Called the "Rule of 72s," this metric approximates (a) the requisite horizon given some return or (b) the requisite return given some horizon. So for a sum to double over an 8-year horizon requires a 9-percent return ($9 \times 8 = 72$). A 6-percent return requires a 12-year horizon ($6 \times 12 = 72$). Table 5.2 illustrates a fuller picture of the relationships.

The Rule of 72s is a rule of thumb. For example, it doesn't work for one-year periods (doubling money in a single year is a 100-percent return for 1 year, for a product of 100). It is only an approximation for other periods. Suppose your money has doubled in 5 years (say you bought a house for $250,000 cash, and 5 years later sold it for $500,000 cash). Using the Rule of 72s indicates a return of 14.4 percent ($5 \times 14.4 = 72$), though using a formal calculation yields 14.87 percent. Table 5.3 shows results of the formal calculations.

It is misleading to conclude that you've generated a 100-percent return on the investment because it took 5 years to get there, not a single year. Nor is it accurate to claim a 20-percent annual return, as by simply dividing 100 percent by 5 years (this is called an arithmetic rate of return and fails to recognize the role of compounding). The rate yielded by the formal equation, and the approximation given by the Rule of 72s, is called the geometric rate of return and captures the force of compounding. (Many refer to this as the CAGR, for compound annual growth rate.)

The Rule of 72s and Table 5.1 assume annual compounding. More frequent compounding implies higher future values. Long-run differ-

Table 5.2 Doubling Periods

	3	4	5.1	6	7.2	8	9	10.2	12	14.4
24	•									
18		•								
14			•							
12				•						
10					•					
9						•				
8							•			
7								•		
6									•	
5										•

ences are staggering. For example, monthly compounding of $1000 at 25 percent over 40 years yields $20 million versus $7.5 million using annual compounding. Less extreme combinations reveal meaningful differences: The future value of $1000 at 15 percent for 10 years is 10-percent greater using monthly versus annual compounding.

The joys of compounding and the 72 rule of thumb follow from more basic insights concerning the time value of money. The adage says a dollar in hand is worth more than a dollar in the future. The steps used to calculate the difference are called discounting.

The intuition and math are simple. If you deposit $1 in a bank account bearing 8-percent annual interest, the dollar grows to $1.08 in one year's time. That means $1 today is equivalent to $1.08 a year later and that $1.08 a year later is worth $1 today. The math: $1 × (1 + .08) = $1.08 and $1.08 / (1 + .08) = $1. Likewise, $.93 today will grow to $1 in a year, and $1 in a year is worth $.93 today.

The relationship is clear: $1 in hand grows in value according to the interest rate; $1 receivable in the future shrinks in value according to the discount rate. The difference in each case is attributable partly to inflation and partly to compensate the investor for surrendering present dollars to future payment.

Taking a further step, into compounding, $1 two years later is worth geometrically more. It grows according to the math: $1 × (1 + .08) × (1 + .08). That yields a future value for the dollar of $1.164 (not merely $1.16). Flipped around, a dollar receivable in two years is worth geometrically less: $1 / (1 + .08) × (1 + .08). That equals $0.857.

Table 5.3 Results of Formal Calculations

So future dollars are worth less in present value terms the longer we have to wait to receive payment. For investors surrendering funds, the rate of difference is called the rate of return; for those accepting funds, it is called the cost of capital.

The illustrated math can be put in a general symbolic form. The following says that the present value (*PV*) of $1 is determined by multiplying the dollar by a discount factor equal to 1 divided by 1 plus the interest rate (called *R*), expounded to the number of years until payment is received (designated as ^{t}):

Following is a built-up equation:

$$PV = \$1 \times \left(\frac{1}{1 + R} \right)^t$$

Simplifying, the picture can be rewritten as follows:
Following is a built-up equation:

$$PV = \frac{\$1}{(1 + R)^t}$$

This formula can be used to calculate the present value of any future cash flow stream, whether from bonds, stocks, royalties and patent licenses or other assets. Take a simple example concerning a bond with a face amount of $1000 paying interest for 10 years and a 100-percent return of principal at year 10. Suppose the annual payment is $80 and the appropriate discount rate is 8 percent (this pair of assumptions means the bond is being sold at "par value"—that is, at an interest rate equal to the discount rate).

A discount factor must be applied to each annual payment, $80 in years 1 through 9, and $1080 for year 10. As described above, the first annual payment is subject to a discount factor equal to (1 / 1.08), meaning a discount factor of .93 and thus has a present value of $74.07. The second annual payment is discounted at 1 / 1.08 × 1.08, for a discount factor of .86 and thus a present value of $68.59. Discounting each future payment and adding them up produces a present value for the stream of payments equal to $1000.

The bond's value changes during its life if interest rates for similar financial instruments change. If comparable rates rise to 9 percent, for example, the payment streams would be revalued using that rate in the discount factor. This would reduce the present value of the future cash flows and thus the value of the bond. The intuition: You can generate 9 percent in alternative investments, so an instrument yielding a comparatively lower 8 percent is worth less.

When comparable interest rates rise, a bond's price should fall. What willing investors will pay for the bond should be no greater than the present value of the future stream of cash flows, properly discounted. The difference between what investors pay for an instrument and the present value of its cash flows is called the investment's net present value.

Rational investors never allocate capital to instruments bearing negative net present values. In perfect economic markets, instruments are always bought and sold at prices resulting in net present values equal to zero. The key point for value investing is that value investors never allocate capital to investments bearing other than positive net present values.

Investors trading at prices for values that equate net present value to zero enjoy the market return. Those finding investments offering positive net present values enjoy an advantage. The spread offers a final dramatization of the combined power of compounding with successful value investing.

Suppose the market return is 10 percent, the return expected by investors always trading at price-value metrics where net present value is zero. Table 5.4 shows results for departures below and above that level, with the market return in between. The five lines below the market return show incremental advantages to investors enjoying superior compounded annual returns over various time horizons. The five above show the opposite. (Figures are again rounded to dramatize the substantial differences.)

Settling for the market return is fine. Dipping below its return is destructive. Edging it out by even seemingly small margins such as 2 percent drives enormous value. For a 10-year horizon, steady advantages of 2 percent ahead of the market produce a total return more than 10 percent greater. These compelling differences are among value investing's strongest attractions and reasons for its success.

Table 5.4 Getting Beaten by or Beating the Market

	1 YR.	*5 YRS.*	*10 YRS.*	*20 YRS.*	*40 YRS.*
0	1,000	1,000	1,000	1,000	1,000
2%	1,020	1,100	1,220	1,500	2,200
4%	1,040	1,200	1,480	2,200	4,800
6%	1,060	1,350	1,790	3,200	10,300
8%	1,080	1,500	2,160	4,700	21,700
10%	**1,100**	**1,600**	**2,600**	**6,700**	**45,000**
12%	1,120	1,800	3,100	9,600	93,000
14%	1,140	1,925	3,700	13,700	189,000
16%	1,160	2,100	4,400	19,500	379,000
18%	1,180	2,300	5,200	27,400	750,000
20%	1,200	2,500	6,200	38,300	1.5 million

CHAPTER 6

VALUE MEASUREMENTS

The value of any asset (stock, bond, business, or other) is a function of the cash inflows and outflows, discounted at an appropriate rate, that an investor can reasonably expect it to generate during its remaining life. Bond values are easiest to measure. Standard bonds bear a designated interest rate and a set maturity date. The combination defines expected cash flows and appropriate discount rate.

Common stocks have no such coupon, and their life is perpetual. An analyst thus must estimate both components of the valuation exercise. Another crucial difference is that qualitative variables such as managerial probity and skill have a direct bearing on common stock values, but a limited effect on bond values.

In selecting investments, value investors choose those shown by valuation analysis to be the cheapest. Valuation analysis takes account of all relevant business factors, including financial strength, relative business growth, and steadiness of earnings. Once a valuation estimate is made, no additional consideration should be given to such factors.

Hunting for good investment prospects entails assessing only the group of companies most likely to win the valuation contest. Among these businesses are those ablest to deploy additional capital at high rates of return compared to capital costs. Businesses to avoid are those that must employ additional capital at low rates of return compared to capital costs. The former population is far smaller than the latter.

Applying the valuation equation to this universe of companies is difficult and poses substantial risk of error. To minimize error risk, value investing calls for a key disciplining attitude: margin of safety. It prescribes never paying a price approximately equal to (or greater than) the value estimate you've made. If the investor is wrong, he will lose. If the investor insists on paying only a fraction of any value estimate she makes, even if she is wrong, she may avoid future losses and certainly will reduce them.

While all investors agree that intrinsic worth is the present value of cash that an asset generates for its owner, serious disagreement arises concerning the factors used to estimate cash flows and the relevant discount rate. Debate concerning cash flows focuses on what data most reliably indicate this value. Cash flows are pictures of the future, and gauging the future can only be done by drawing on the past.

Which historical indicators are the best gauges of future performance? Candidates include historical cash flows themselves, recent earnings history, and existing asset and liability levels. Even among prominent value investors, emphasis varies concerning which gauges are best suited for valuation exercises. All agree that in order of importance, analysis must focus on the balance sheet, the income statement, and the cash flow statement.

BALANCE SHEET VALUE: ASSETS AT WORK

Pure value investing starts with the balance sheet, the list of assets and liabilities, and the resulting difference called book value. Three metrics can be derived: net asset value, liquidation value, and reproduction cost. In some areas, our economic environment has outpaced our accounting principles so that sizable asset classes called intangibles bearing large values remain unrecorded on the asset side of a balance sheet. Examples are intellectual property (copyrights, patents, and trademarks) and human capital (a well-trained workforce, know-how, and specialized skill sets).

Nevertheless, value investing requires analyzing the balance sheet. The most conservative form of value investing examines solely current assets, subtracts all liabilities, and estimates the difference as the company's value. Graham made this famous as the net-net working capital figure. It is somewhat impractical, however, for few companies today operate using current assets that are greater than total liabilities.

A key insight about Graham and value investing endures, however: One reason for this focus relates to the data's reliability. Current assets are the most reliable of all financial data. Valuation data become more unreliable as one moves (a) down the balance sheet from cash into longer-term current assets and into long-term assets, (b) into the income statement and down it, and (c) onto the cash flow statement.

Balance sheet data become less reliable for valuation because items tend to be more firm- or industry-specific:

- Every business can use cash so a dollar held is pretty much worth a dollar.

- Accounts receivable are generally more easily collected by the company that generated them, but they can be assigned or sold, and the buyer can collect most of what the company could (this commonly occurs by the process of factoring in the textile industry for example).

- Inventory can be used only by other merchandisers or manufacturers in the same or similar industries.

- Property, plant, and equipment may be less adaptable even by peers, or can be illiquid.

- Goodwill is all but unique to a firm (other intangible assets such as trademarks, patents, and copyrights typically don't appear on the balance sheet).

Liquidation value is the net realizable amount that could be generated by selling a company's assets and discharging all its liabilities. When valuing a business for liquidation, most assets are marked down and the liabilities treated at face value. Cash and securities are taken at face value. Receivables require a small discount (perhaps 15 percent to 25 percent off), inventory a larger discount (perhaps 50 percent to 75 percent off), and fixed assets at least as much as inventory. Any goodwill should probably be ignored, as should most intangible assets and prepaid expenses.

The residual is the shareholders' take. This valuation method is useful for companies being dissolved. It doesn't consider value arising from deploying the resources in combination. It is thus of limited use for valuing businesses as going concerns.

For a going concern, three asset valuation approaches are recognized. Graham's was the most stringent, consisting of measuring current assets and subtracting from them all liabilities. If the target is selling for less than that difference, a sizable margin of safety exists. Such results are as rare as hen's teeth today.

Another alternative is book value, pure and simple. That is, if a company can be bought for a per-share price equal to less than the difference between its reported total assets and reported total liabilities, it probably furnishes a comfortable margin of safety as well. While such companies sometimes exist in contemporary corporate America, they too are not common. Also, value investing inclines some skepticism towards reported figures, justifying consideration of the third method of asset valuation called the reproduction cost method.

In the reproduction cost method of balance sheet valuation, the concept is to value a going concern on the basis of what it would take a new entrant to its business to build it from scratch at current costs or replacement value. All a target's resources and claims against it are separately assessed and netted out. The cash, securities, receivables, and inventory probably can be taken at face value, as can prepaid expenses.

Investigation is required to ensure that receivables have been adequately reserved through the allowance for bad debt accounts, and that inventory accounting is neither overstated (due to aging that suggests they are nonsalable for example) nor understated (due to inflation in sales prices compared to historical records concerning the cost of those goods held for sale). Fixed assets should be adjusted to reflect current market conditions, compared to the historical prices (net of depreciation) at which they are carried on the books. Accounting goodwill remains an asset class warranting little valuation accretion.

In addition to assets appearing on a going concern's balance sheet, numerous resources bearing value do not appear under GAAP. These so-called hidden assets include brand-name identity, product qualities, know-how, employee training, and specialized production and distribution arrangements.

For example, a new entrant might need to invest in research and development (R&D) to replicate the target company. This exact value is difficult to estimate. An informed guess can be made by estimating the life cycle of the resulting product and multiplying this by the target's average annual level of R&D expense. For a patented pharmaceutical, for example, product life could be up to the 17-year life of a patent. So if the company spends 5 percent annually on R&D for its patented products, an amount equal to about 85 percent of current revenues would be warranted.

Similar estimating is appropriate to value customer relationships. These take time and resources to build. They may be judged by some multiple of the target's annual selling and administrative expenses— perhaps between one and three years' worth of these. Additional estimating goes into other hidden assets such as governmental licenses, franchise agreements, and other valuable resources that are not listed on a balance sheet under standard accounting rules.

The liabilities of a going concern, taken at face value, are subtracted from assessment in the reproduction cost method of valuation.

Judgment is required for certain liability classes, however, such as for deferred tax liabilities or contingencies. A new entrant would not necessarily face such obligations. If not, they may be omitted. Debt, however, should be subtracted, either at its carrying amount or its market value, whichever is higher.

Analyzing the balance sheet includes assessing the level of liabilities and determining whether all liabilities are properly recorded. It is also prudent to examine the relationship between recorded depreciation over time and capital reinvestment levels. The former is a proxy for the latter; as a proxy, it must be tested to determine whether actual reinvestment needs are more or less than recorded depreciation expenses.

The figures resulting from analyzing the balance sheet remain baselines. The company is worth at least the net of its total assets less total liabilities. Whether it is worth a premium depends on its ability to leverage the asset base through competitive advantages that result in barriers to entry that keep competitors out.

INCOME STATEMENT VALUE: THE EARNINGS PAYOFF

Successful asset leveraging shows up in the income statement. The income statement reports revenues less expenses and depicts an important measure of business performance. This is not a picture of cash flows because GAAP uses accrual, not a cash method of reporting.

In accrual accounting, economic activity is recorded according to the relationship between revenue and expense, rather than the timing of cash inflows or outflows. This is not an idiosyncrasy of accounting tradition, but a reflection of accounting's goal of measuring and allocating business events that reflect economic reality. Those accruals capturing noncash costs of doing business reflect that cash will be absorbed in the future.

Pure value investors (Graham and Dodd) believe that current earnings (adjusted as discussed below) are the most reliable indicator of a company's sustainable long-term cash flows. Adding a further constraint, pure value investors believe that the most reliable way to use current earnings as a valuation metric is to assume they will be constant in the future at current rates—not grow according to estimates.

The math is easy. Valuation based on current earnings is equal to current earnings divided by the company's current cost of capital (that is, $V = E/k$). The virtues of this approach are simplicity and reliability: Both data points are known or can be reliably estimated. Earnings are earnings; the cost of capital is the company's weighted average cost of debt and cost of equity (the former can be calculated simply; the latter still requires some estimating as discussed in the next chapter). Characteristic of simplicity is that investors need not bother with growth rates because no growth is assumed.

Apart from estimating the cost of equity capital, earnings-based valuation relies on some accounting judgments to confirm the integrity of current earnings. The exercise may call for adjustments in the reported figures to render the current earnings figure the best estimate of the company's sustainable long-term cash flows.

Among justifications for adjusting current earnings is the distortion caused by one-time charges. Companies sometimes bury bad news affecting multiple years into a single charge and dismiss the result as a nonrecurring episode. Adjusting for this practice requires reallocating the one-time charge across multiple periods and adjusting the current year's earnings accordingly.

Other justifications for adjusting current earnings are accounting allocations for noncash charges such as depreciation and amortization. These are intended to serve as a proxy for how close a company's capital assets are drawing to the ends of their useful lives and must be replaced. It is common for the required reinvestment in such capital assets to exceed the amount allocated in the accounting.

Current earnings may also be adjusted to the extent that the current year is an aberration for substantive economic reasons. If the year is a cyclical down year for the company, an upward adjustment based on earnings of prior years is indicated; if at a boom in the corporate or industrial business cycle, the reverse would be true.

Value investing eschews *pro forma* financial figures. These are pictures of performance based on making various assumptions other than those applied in preparing actual financial statements. While useful for certain exercises such as depicting how a newly merged company would have looked if the merger had occurred some years earlier, they do not represent useful valuation resources in other contexts. *Pro forma* figures are the least reliable data in financial reporting and are invariably unreliable for a valuation exercise.

Also suspect for pure value investors are assumptions about growth in future earnings extrapolated from current or past earnings. Unlike extreme devotees of growth investing, value investors consider current earnings—adjusted as described—to be the best estimate of sustainable future cash flows. A key reason to deny estimated and unknown earnings growth is that absent sustainable competitive advantages or barriers to competitor entry, growth lacks value.

If new entrants can join a company's industry as equal competitors, the effect drives a company's returns to just equal their costs—no upside is sustainable so growth adds nothing. Growing a business measured in sales requires growing the business measured in assets. Growing assets requires capital, which also poses a cost. Facing competitive entrants, the process goes nowhere (except remotely due to luck and temporarily—benefits value investors do not pay for).

FRANCHISE VALUE

Another reason for pure value investing's aversion to valuations based on growth estimates is that growth's potential value can be ascertained using other accounting tools not requiring estimates. This involves comparing valuation estimates using earnings with those using assets.

Three possibilities arise: The valuations are the same or one or the other is higher. When they are the same, growth bears no value as just noted. When asset value exceeds earnings value, managers are deploying assets suboptimally, either due to ineptitude or excess industry capacity. No value resides there.

When earnings value exceeds asset value, it is due to competitive advantages or barriers to entry, and these clues indicate potential value in growth. This indicates a company possessing franchise value. One measure of that value is the excess of earnings value over asset value. It is captured in the expression return on equity. This economic goodwill makes companies value investor candidates.

Franchise businesses are those boasting barriers to entry and other competitive advantages that make it too costly for new entrants to join. Strong brands can help, so long as competitors cannot match them. Examples include at least for some period of time those products bearing names synonymous with the goods, such as Coke, Kleenex, Hoover (in its day), Harley-Davidson (to some extent), and others.

Techniques producing franchise value include patents, exclusive licenses, know-how, and secret formulae. Generally high fixed-costs of entry also help. Common elements of franchise businesses include high costs to consumers of switching away from the target's own product in favor of products sold by competitors, high costs to consumers of seeking out such alternatives, and habits commanding consumer loyalty.

Foes of the franchise power are constraints competitors can evade. Examples are a unionized labor force, burdensome distribution arrangements, or limitations on an entity's adaptability in the face of change.

GROWTH'S VALUE

Growth is not free. Its price is the cost of capital necessary to support it. Growth adds value only when the return on capital exceeds the cost of capital. Take an example drawn from Bruce Greenwald's detailed book on value investing.

Suppose that earnings are $32. An analyst determines it would cost $20 to grow earnings by 10 percent forever. So you can have either $32 forever or $12 growing at 10 percent forever. Which is better, no-growth or growth? It depends on the cost of capital.

Use the following standard valuation formula:

$$V = \frac{D_1}{k - g}$$

This formula is a variation on that mentioned when discussing current earnings, giving effect to same rate of growth designated by g.

Comparing our example, assume $k = 20\%$ and $g = 0$ or 10%. Then:

(a) $V = \dfrac{32}{.20 - 0} = \$160$

(b) $V = \dfrac{12}{.20 - .10} = \$120$

With a 20-percent cost of capital, $32 forever is better than $12 growing at 10 percent forever. Thus, growth subtracts value when the cost of capital exceeds the return on capital.

Assume instead $k = 14\%$. Then:

(a) $V = \dfrac{32}{.14 - 0} = \$229$

(b) $V = \dfrac{12}{.14 - .10} = \$300$

With a 20-percent cost of capital, $32 forever is better than $12 growing at 10 percent forever. Thus, growth adds value when the return on capital exceeds the cost of capital.

Assume finally $k = 16\%$. Then:

(a) $V = \dfrac{32}{.16 - 0} = \$200$

(b) $V = \dfrac{12}{.16 - .10} = \$200$

Growth is neutral to value when the cost of capital equals the return on capital.

This illustration proves the powerful insight: When capital costs equal capital returns, growth neither adds nor subtracts value, no matter how much or how little growth there is. The reason is intuitive: If an investor putting in new capital charges the same rate that capital generates, then there is no additional return available to prior investors.

To come full circle, growth is not free. If a company can attract capital at a cost lower than returns it generates, growth adds value. If it attracts capital at a cost higher than what it generates, growth subtracts value. If the cost of capital is the same as the return on capital, growth is neutral to value.

The only businesses in the first category are those possessing franchise characteristics. The only way to capture returns on capital greater than the cost of capital is to keep competitors out. If competitors can get in, capital costs and returns will soon converge upon each other (or worse, capital costs will exceed capital returns).

Before turning to examining cash-flow based valuation techniques, note two crucial points captured in Figure 6.1's image: (1) assets drive earnings and cash flows and (2) assets are analytically more important than either. As to point (1), for most businesses, asset value exceeds earnings value; businesses whose earnings value exceeds asset value possess franchise characteristics. This implies the ability to sustain high returns on equity (high earnings relatives to net assets). As to point (2), data reliability varies. Balance sheet data tend to be most reliable for valuation exercises, then income statement data concerning current earnings. Properly estimated cash flows are probably less than earnings, though many contemporary analysts draw the opposite conclusion by ignoring important noncash charges to income such as depreciation.

DISCOUNTED CASH FLOW ANALYSIS: HIGH SUBJECTIVITY

The reason value investing emphasizes the balance sheet and income statement is that to resort solely to the cash flow statement can be deceptively simple. Cash flows alone disguise important metrics. Cash is not exactly the bottom line. True, cash flows drive value, but some portion of cash flows will be needed to reinvest in capital resources

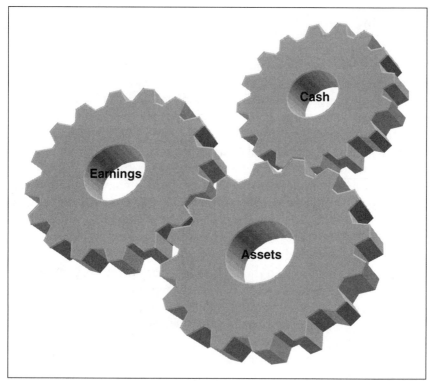

Figure 6.1. Value Drivers.

necessary to sustain business production and results. Thus to arrive at a cash flow figure by adjusting net income for noncash expenditures is only a partial step. Step two is to further adjust that figure by probable future cash commitments to capital expenditures.

Suppose a company generates net income of $1 million. Part of the expenses recorded to generate the $1 million consisted of net noncash charges of $200,000. Cash flow is thus $1.2 million. That is step one. Then this figure must be adjusted to reflect the amount the company will need to disburse in cash to maintain its property, plant, and equipment at levels sufficient to sustain business productivity. Suppose this figure is either $.1 million or $.3 million. Adjusted, cash flows are now either $.9 million or $1.1 million. This is the bottom line figure, and may be called free cash flows. (Buffett calls it owner earnings to designate that these are the free flows of results allocable to the common stock.)

Too often analysts fail to take this additional step of adjusting for the probable costs of required reinvestment. It would be more accurate for these analysts simply to stick with the net income figure. After all, the noncash charges to earnings that produce the net income figure are at least, in part, intended as a proxy to estimate such required reinvestment. In this example, the bookkeeping allocation of noncash charges of $.2 million may be as reasonable an estimate of required cash reinvestment as the separate estimates of either $.1 million or $.3 million. But zeroing in on this figure is a crucial value investing exercise.

Despite these points about cash flows, the most popular contemporary approach to valuation emphasizes cash flows pure and simple. Called discounted cash flow (DCF) analysis, the method also presents a number of choices an analyst must make.

Cash flows can be measured in alternative ways. Chief examples are operating income (earnings before interest and taxes, called EBIT) and operating income plus the noncash expenses of depreciation and amortization (called EBITDA). Devotees of discounted cash flow valuation analysis rarely use accounting-driven metrics such as operating income.

Once cash flows are defined using one of these metrics, the discounted cash flow valuation method estimates them for a medium-term period, typically 5 to 10 years. The estimate entails examining a range of performance variables that drive cash flows, chiefly sales levels, profit margins, and required reinvestment in the business through capital expenditures (cap-ex). With cash flows projected, the method discounts each year's estimate by a discount rate intended to reflect the subject company's cost of capital during the period. Each year's discounted result is added to all others to produce a preliminary valuation of the 5- or 10-year period.

For cash flows beyond the medium term, an additional step estimates the further cash expected in perpetuity, at a constant growing rate. This is typically done by estimating the final year's cash flows and multiplying it by some figure to yield the perpetuity amount. The figure is determined by the relationship between the assumed growth rate and the relevant cost of capital at that horizon period. It is equal to 1 divided by the difference between these rates—so with a cost of capital of 10 percent and a growth rate of 5 percent, the multiplier is 20 determined by 1/(10 percent – 5 percent).

The requisite math is elegant, easy, superficially scientific and seemingly objective. The raw data is estimated, just as easily, but substantially artistic and actually subjective. Underscore the heroics: cash flows estimated for 5 or 10 years, cash flows in perpetuity, discount rates going out 10 years plus, and a growth rate on top of that in perpetuity.

The process of estimation and discounting is intended to recognize the hazards of the future by incorporating into the cash flow estimates the onslaughts of competition, technology, patent expiration, deregulation, globalization, and other upheaval. This entails close examination of factors such as sales, margins, and cap-ex. Likewise, the discount rate is intended to capture the effects on capital costs of long-term financing markets, lender appetites for the company's securities, and all such underlying risks. (These are discussed in the next chapter.)

But all these variables are by definition unknown, uncertain, and difficult to quantify. In the math, moreover, tiny differences in the assumptions drive substantial differences in resulting valuations. Among the largest component of resulting value in this model is the value assigned to the horizon (the perpetuity piece beyond the 5- or 10-year mark). Its derivation is a function of assumed growth rate and assumed cost of capital. At estimates of 5 percent and 10 percent, as noted, the multiple is 20; tweak these and enormous ranges emerge.

Even so, the discounted cash flow valuation model is the most widespread model in contemporary valuation. Some value investors use it, at least in part. Others eschew it entirely. Both groups look instead to assets and earnings measures deemed more reliable than cash flows to come to grips with valuation.

C H A P T E R   7

DISCOUNT RATES

Choosing an appropriate discount rate (or cost of capital) is necessary to determine present value, whether measured by current earnings or a more elaborate discounted cash flow model. The discount rate must reflect the time value of money and the specific risks associated with the individual company. Equity is riskier than debt, so the discount rate for a given company will be some increment above the prevailing rates at which any debt it has outstanding are being discounted. The challenge is determining how much greater.

Conceptually, think of the discount rate as the rate of return a prudent investor would require for allocating capital to the subject company. A high-risk venture would warrant a proportionately high discount rate; a sure thing, a rate probably equal to the time value of money. The surest investments in contemporary investing are U.S. government securities. These furnish the risk-free rate.

Appropriate discount rates for most corporate equity will take U.S. government securities as the starting point and add an additional element. Considered below are two alternative conceptual approaches to thinking about and settling upon an appropriate discount rate, one traditional and one from modern finance theory.

VALUE INVESTING APPROACH TO RISK AND RATES

The "risk-free rate" can be estimated by reference to U.S. government securities, loans investors make to the U.S. Treasury. The U.S. Treasury is seen as the purest credit risk in the world, committed to paying its debts when due without fail. Hence, yields on U.S. Treasury debt are considered the benchmark for valuing all other assets, including corporate debt and equities. Corporate debt bears greater risk than U.S. Treasury debt. In corporate bankruptcy, debt is paid before common stock, so the common stock of a company carrying debt bears a greater risk than that debt.

Selecting a risk-free rate requires judgment based on various factors. Such factors include bond maturity, reference date or time frame, and reference source. Possible sources include the rate disclosed in a company's own public filings. This is a nonarbitrary choice, reflecting the rate the company uses for its internal purposes and considered sufficiently material to disclose in its public filings. Other customs include using 30-year bonds to reflect the long-term character of the investment in a corporation.

When valuing a business as a going concern, following the daily, weekly, or monthly movements in the U.S. Treasury market introduces distorting valuation volatility into the exercise. Business value does not move in tandem with daily or even monthly fluctuations in Treasury rates. Avoiding the sensitivity to short-term fluctuations in Treasury rates can be done by averaging rates over the preceding year or so.

To the risk-free is added an amount reflecting risks associated with a particular investment. This produces the discount rate to apply to determine the present value of an asset. For a business with debt and equity in its capital structure, this is commonly called the weighted average cost of capital (WACC). It is the proportional cost of a company's debt, determined by the after-tax interest cost, and the cost of equity, determined by a more judgment-laden but conceptually identical inquiry.

The cost of equity is conceptually identical to the cost of debt because they involve the same question: What must the company pay to induce investment, whether from debt lenders or equity holders? The cost-of-equity exercise is more judgment-laden than the cost-of-debt exercise because there are no maturity dates or set coupons on equity (dividends are payable solely in the corporate board's discretion).

The key reference is what other capital market participants are paying investors to attract equity financing for enterprises of comparable risk. To estimate the cost of equity capital for high-risk venture capital projects, for example, one could consult the returns offered by venture capitalists in such enterprises. For low-risk enterprises, underwritten secondary public offerings of blue-chip companies can be examined.

Most generally, the practice is to estimate the returns investors are insisting upon for companies bearing like qualities (in terms of industry, capital structure, maturation, size, competitive outlook, and so on). For companies with long records of sustained earnings, low rates are indicated, perhaps just a few points above the risk-free rate. For newer, more volatile operations, a larger premium is required.

The estimate requires exercising practical judgment based on learning what compensation is given to investors bearing comparable business and financial risks. What special business and financial risks do common stockholders face? What are the debt levels? What is the likelihood that debt investors would be paid before them or that high debt would throw the company into bankruptcy? What is the company's financial strength and industry leadership? Is its market expanding or contracting? Is there room for growth that will add value?

In short, assessing risk relevant to the discount rate implicates the same questions value investors ask when defining circles of competence (discussed in Chapter 3). Value investors see risk as arising from either deterioration in an investment's business value or overpaying for it in the first place. Overpayment can result from inadequate or mistaken analysis of these questions. The possibility of misrelating price and value implies a commonsense point: High stock prices compared to earnings make for high-risk investments.

A value investor's conception of risk differs from that of modern finance theory, today's dominant model for defining risk. This theory measures risk using market price fluctuations as proxies for underlying business-value changes. While the exercise appears precisely scientific, in fact it is as judgment-laden as the traditional method. It also defies common sense: In this model, the fact that a stock price is high or low compared to earnings has no bearing on risk. Despite these weaknesses, the widespread use of this model warrants summarizing it as a contrast to value investing.

PORTFOLIO THEORY APPROACH: *BETA* AND PREMIUMS

Modern finance theory uses the "capital asset pricing model" (CAPM) to estimate discount rates for equities. Using CAPM requires estimating two inputs in addition to a risk-free rate. These are a "market risk premium" and "*beta*," a measure of stock price volatility seen by backers as a risk indicator. The mistake some analysts make is to assume that there is a single accurate data point for each of these inputs. However, each of these variables is an estimate requiring judgment.

The variables also are integrated so that changes in one may indicate modification of another. For example, increases in the risk-free rate entail decreases in the market risk premium (the latter supposedly measures the difference between the risk-free rate and the expected return on common stocks). The need for estimation judgment, and the complex interrelationship among these variables, means that prudent analysis draws on multiple reasonable data points (by applying alternative methods and taking alternative measures of each variable).

The "market risk premium" is a guess based on history of what special inducements it takes to attract investors into stocks rather than buying U.S. Treasury securities or alternative investments. The idea is that investors must be given special compensation to bear the special risks of stocks or else they will not invest in them.

Common practice is to consult data books published by leading economists, such as the one published by a firm run by Yale University professor Roger Ibbotson called the *Ibbotson & Sinquefeld Yearbook*. The harder way is doing it yourself, which is virtually impossible for nonprofessionals. But it is useful to understand why, so here goes.

Market risk premium data can be calculated up-to-the-minute at any time. Three crucial assumptions must be made to estimate the market risk premium. First, the estimator must choose either historical data or some measure of future performance. Second, one must define a "market" for the measure, such as the Standard & Poor's 500, the New York Stock Exchange as a whole, or some other index.

Third, the estimate is based on a specified time period. Alternatives include the period from the late 1800s (when market data were first recorded) to the time of valuation interest; from 1926 (when the University of Chicago began a database, thought to have the virtue of including a full business cycle before the 1929 market crash) to the time of valuation interest; for the 30-year period before the time of valuation interest (reflecting business cycles exhibiting more relevant business and financial risks and factors); or for specific environments being analyzed, such as the early 2000s.

Seizing on a measure of the "market risk premium" became acutely tricky during the late 1990s because any such thing seemed to be evaporating. Any premium that once existed—*e.g.*, in the period before 1990—dwindled toward zero, as the most powerful bull market in world history produced investors who needed no inducements to join. Even staunch devotees of modern finance theory lamented the declining usefulness of the "market risk premium" device during the 1990s.

Despite this well-known fact even among its fans, analysts sticking with this learning adhere to favorite benchmarks, such as 9 percent based on long-run historical returns on stocks dating back to the 1930s. Others respond to their gut sense that this is almost certainly wrong, and opt instead for rates of 7 percent, 5 percent, or less. Some believe it was moving towards zero in the late 1990s.

A group of the country's leading financial economists assembled in mid-2000 to offer their measurements of the market risk premium. Eleven participated. Their estimates of the risk premium were: 0, 1-2, 3, 3-4, 4, 6, 6, and 8.1 percent, with three refusing to venture a guess given the concept's indefiniteness and uncertain reliability.

Reasons for the decline or evaporation include powerful forces, such as U.S. investors became more long-term oriented, U.S. business efficiency heightened, fiscal policies and monetary management improved, capitalism spread globally, wealth increased, and business fundamentals exhibited less volatility. (See Table 7.1.)

As for *beta*, it is intended to reveal what part of any "market risk premium" is borne by a particular company's stock. *Beta* determines this component of the discount rate estimate for a company's equity by using various assumptions to compare its stock price gyrations with those of the overall stock market or a market index such as the S&P 500.

A stock whose price is more volatile than the market's is seen as "riskier" than one whose price gyrates less than the market as a whole. Multiplying this measure of price volatility by a "market risk premium" theoretically expresses the differential risk the particular stock poses. The result is added to the risk-free rate to give a discount rate.

Beta is only potentially useful if stock prices of the subject company and of all components of the market or market index result from investor behavior that is, collectively, rational. Such conditions of "market efficiency" might substantially occur for some companies in some cases and for some markets or some market segments at some times.

Table 7.1 Discount Rate Determinations

	VALUE INVESTING	PORTFOLIO INVESTING
Baseline	Long-term U.S. Treasuries	Long-term U.S. Treasuries
Addition	Risk assessment (conscious judgment)	Market risk premium × *beta* (seemingly scientific)

Value investing and portfolio theory determine discount rates by adding an amount to the risk-free rate ascertained from long-term U.S. Treasury securities. Portfolio theory uses the product of the market risk premium and the target's *beta*. Value investing questions the seemingly scientific quality of this exercise in favor of more judgment-laden but conscious assessments of associated risk.

But these conditions do not always exist. Market pricing and volatility of the late 1990s give reason to believe that these conditions did not exist. Some companies trade at prices bearing a discount from their intrinsic value—the key claim of value investing. Numerous other flaws infect *beta*, widely documented in a burgeoning literature over the past decade showing its declining utility.

General faith in *beta* requires general faith in efficient markets. But belief in efficient markets means the equity risk premium in the late 1990s was negative, zero, or very close to zero—that is the only way to make sense of the high stock prices prevalent in the late 1990s if markets are efficient. Under CAPM, a zero-market-risk premium implies a discount rate equal to the risk-free rate. But this is a strange result, defying common sense that common stocks are riskier than U.S. Treasuries.

We are back to where we started: Estimating appropriate discount rates for equity securities requires judgment about how much riskier a particular business is compared to risk-free benchmarks of U.S. Treasuries. Modern finance theory assumes return is correlated to risk (you get what you pay for); value investing understands return as correlated to effort (you get what you deserve).

CHAPTER 8

MARKET PRICES

Value investing works if stock prices fluctuate around business value. Only then can stocks be bought at discounts to business value (or sold at premiums to business value). Value investors believe that markets price stocks in ways that produce such gaps. Graham's metaphor described this behavior as Mr. Market, viewing market action as the collective psychological behavior of human beings prone to periods of excessive optimism and pessimism. The conception yields several insights for what value investing is.

FACTORS

Numerous complex factors influence stock market prices. Graham identified two categories of factors: speculative and investment. Speculative factors are the jungle of the marketplace and include technical aspects of market trading as well as manipulative and psychological ones. Investment factors relate to valuation, principally assessments of financial data, including earnings and assets. See Figure 8.1.

Factors sharing traits of both the marketplace and valuations, which Graham called future value factors, include managerial qualities, competitive circumstances, and a company's outlook for sales and profit. All of these factors are filtered through the lens of the investing public's attitude, which produces trading decisions and bids and offers in the market. The output is market price.

The idea that anyone can predict the outcome of this process, or that it works in a way that yields prices just equal to value, is farfetched. Value investing considers trying to measure market sentiment a waste of time. Value investing focuses primarily on business value, not market price.

Emphasizing businesses over prices enables value investors to know that owning stock means owning an interest in a going concern. That

Figure 8.1. Graham's Depiction of the Relationship of Intrinstic Value to Market Price

I. *General market factors.*
II. *Individual factors.*

A. Speculative

1. Market factors
   - *a.* Technical.
   - *b.* Manipulative.
   - *c.* Psychological.

2. Future value factors
   - *a.* Management and reputation.
   - *b.* Competitive conditions and prospects.
   - *c.* Possible and probable changes in volume, price, and costs.

B. Investment

3. Intrinsic value factors
   - *a.* Earnings.
   - *b.* Dividends.
   - *c.* Assets.
   - *d.* Capital structure.
   - *e.* Terms of the issue.
   - *f.* Others.

Attitude of public toward the issue.

Bids and offers. } Market price

Source: Benjamin Graham & David L. Dodd, *Security Analysis* (2d ed. 1940), page 27.

mental quality promotes the discipline necessary to define a circle of competence, do financial analysis, and assess value-price relationships. Pervasive market price data makes it harder for equity investors to appreciate that they are part owners of a business, making disciplined analysis elusive.

The only reason to consider market sentiment is because in times of general economic despair and market malaise, the odds of successful stock picking rise. Three factors contribute: (1) there are more companies likely to be priced below value, (2) there are fewer investment competitors likely to wade into the thicket, and (3) the media and regulatory pressure tend to promote quality management and conservative accounting.

DOING LITTLE WITH MARKET PRICE

The most-quoted metric in discussing common stocks is their ratio of price-to-earnings (P/E). This states the relationship between what a stock costs and what benefit it produces. Many people wrongly believe that value investing involves finding companies boasting low P/E multiples. But not all low P/E stocks are good investments, and not all high P/E stocks are bad investments. Nor do value investors consider the P/E ratio as an insightful measure for valuation purposes, though it might be useful as a check against overpaying.

The P/E ratio can be used as a screen. Graham avoided buying stocks unless they were priced at their lowest P/E level during the prior five years. He also required an earnings-return compared to price (current earnings divided by price) at least twice that prevailing on high-grade corporate bonds. Other value investors follow these practices. The devices protect against the whims of the marketplace. The market might not be right, but this approach limits the value investor's exposure from it being wrong.

Value investors resist the temptation to use P/E ratios as supplements to a traditional valuation analysis. This contrasts with devotees of pure DCF analysis in valuation exercises. When the latter's results show a wide range of plausible valuations, they often appeal to the P/E ratios of comparable companies as a way to narrow the range.

The approach compares the price of comparable companies to their respective cash flows (P/CF). Suppose a comparable company's P/CF ratio is 10 (suppose a price of 20 and cash flows of 2). That ratio of 10 is then applied to the subject company. Say its cash flows are 3. Its implied comparables-based value is 30. How much this helps is uncertain. The effort relies entirely on the quality of market pricing for the comparable company. While many finance professionals employ the technique, most value investors do not consider it useful.

Value investors consider the income statement and the balance sheet as sources of information concerning business value. These are superior to market-oriented tools such as the P/E ratio for two reasons. First, return on equity captures the full accounting picture, including debt and equity, whereas P/E severs earnings from the balance sheet. Second, return on equity is an intrinsic or internal valuation methodology, whereas P/E ratios are products of market or external or valuation processes. Market metrics tell value investors more about Graham's Mr. Market than about intrinsic value.

RATIONAL THINKING ABOUT IRRATIONAL PRICING

Depressed investors cause depressed stock market prices. Selling pressure mounts and drives prices down. Investors possessing even modest degrees of aversion to loss capitulate quickly, and the less fearsome succumb soon after. A downward market spiral ensues.

Value investors avoid these scenarios by forming a clear assessment of their averseness to loss. Only having assessed this characteristic honestly do they brave the choppy waters of stock picking.

One way to grasp one's own loss aversion is to recognize that most people experience the pain of loss as a multiple compared to the joy of gain. The average person greets losses with aversion on the order of about 2.5 times their reception of winnings. The greater one's loss aversion, the greater value investing's appeal. For the most acutely loss-averse investors, pure value investing is most suitable (Graham was extremely risk averse).

THE ANXIETY OF SELLING

A vexing question facing investors during market sell-offs is whether to join the pack. For value investors, the answer is no, but the more pertinent question is when to sell. Value investors set selling criteria at the time of purchase. Their attitude in buying is to select stocks that are least likely ever to trigger the criteria for selling.

But businesses change, and when they deteriorate, their shares should be sold, just as the owner of a business sometimes must decide to close down. When selecting stocks, value investors specify what deterioration means for purposes of selling. The logic is simple: The same factors used to select and avoid stocks are used to decide which stocks to sell and when.

Sales are indicated when the key factors supporting an original buy are gone. Here is a summary of such factors:

Internal: dubious management behavior, vague disclosure or complex accounting, aggressively increased merger activity, dizzying executive compensation packages.

External: intensifying new competition, disruptive technological onslaughts, deregulation, declining inventory and receivables turns.

Economic: shrunken profit margins; declining returns on equity, assets, and investment; earnings erosion; debt increased aggressively in relation to equity; deterioration in current and quick ratios.

Value investors avoid selling when bad news is temporary. Single-quarter profit margin slippage should provoke questions, but not sales orders. If investigation shows deeper problems, then the condition might be permanent and selling indicated. Permanent deterioration requires more evidence.

When in doubt concerning whether deterioration is temporary or permanent, value investing might include a hedging strategy. This would call for selling some but less than all shares held.

Value investors never sell solely due to falling prices. They require some evidence related to the declining intrinsic value of the business to warrant a revision in the hold-or-sell calculus. Stock price fluctuations are far too fickle to influence such an important decision.

In the case of a preset policy to sell when price reaches a certain high level, many value investors follow the same mixed strategy adhered to when unsure whether a development is permanent or temporary: selling some, but not all.

CONTROL'S VALUE

Value investing discussions invariably begin by noting that intrinsic worth is the discounted cash flows of an asset, without pausing to define the asset. The process is relatively straightforward for assets such as government bonds, a family-owned pizza shop, or a gold mine. It is trickier for common stock.

In the case of common stock, the asset is either the company or the specific stock. The difference concerns the control value associated with owning 100 percent of the stock compared to a single share or other minority interest.

A medium-sized company with 1 million shares outstanding might spin off $100 million in excess cash this year. Each share is theoretically entitled to $100. That could be the basis of a valuation of ownership of that company for this year. But takeover investors interested in buying the entire company will often bid more than $100 million to buy it. In valuation disputes brought by minority shareholders, courts will often add an analogous premium.

Markets tend to price individual shares as if they are minority shares. To value a share of stock, therefore, requires valuing both the business as a whole and the individual share. The price must be compared to both. The result might be that the company valuation is $100 while the price is $90. That does not automatically mean the stock is underpriced and therefore a value investment option. A built-in discount arises in market trading.

Therefore a bigger margin of safety is warranted. This is one of many factors that drove Graham's margin of safety principle. On the other hand, a well-developed takeover market emerged in the decades since Graham pioneered his method. Takeover investors are willing to pay high market premiums and thus return to individual holders a sizable control premium.

Some value investors treat takeover prospects as catalysts to realize value from an investment. For nonprofessional investors, however, betting on takeovers is even more difficult than the general habit of seeking franchise businesses at margin-of-safety prices.

CHAPTER 9

FRAUDS AND FANTASIES

In the late 1990s, all investors except value investors were burned (and the latter performed reasonably well in the early 1990s). Investor classes fooled by the bubble encompassed those dubbed momentum investors, growth investors, index investors, and the portfolio investors of modern finance theory. Value investors avoid fraud and fantasia, the forces that interact to create financial bubbles. They do this by focusing on fundamentals of balance sheet analysis and reliable data about earnings and returns on equity. They do not succumb to machinations that draw attention to other financial metrics and storytelling unrelated to actual, measurable performance. Glaring examples from the late 1990s/early 2000s boom are instructive.

THE HEADY LATE 1990s

The late 1990s boasted economic expansion and technological innovation of a magnitude that comes once a generation in American business. Extraordinary change was led by the exploitation of technologies enabling the widespread use of the Internet and proliferation of telecom infrastructure. To give one practical illustration of the sea change, in 1996 hardly anyone used e-mail and a minority used cell phones; by 2000, a majority used both regularly.

Heady financial times such as these invariably attract to investing millions of people who lack business knowledge and to business thousands of people who lack moral scruples. The combination produces and sustains exaggeration of real achievements and obfuscation of setbacks. Recasting Federal Reserve Chairman Alan Greenspan's diagnosis of the era, there are supply and demand curves for fantasy through phony accounting that intersect where irrational exuberance meets infectious greed. Only value investors pierce these distortions.

Hallucinations of the late 1990s came to an end in the early 2000s, when nonvalue investors finally recognized that a financial bubble had arisen and stock market indexes plunged. The unraveling of Enron Corp., a direct product of the era's financial fantasia, began in late 2001 and escalated in early 2002, heightening already high marketplace anxiety. As the Enron shenanigans unfolded, an accounting meltdown at Global Crossing, Ltd. was unveiled. Dubious financial reporting concerning a wide range of practices and policies surfaced at the telecom industry's darling.

A wave of reported corporate debacles followed in mid-2002, featuring marquee telecom firms WorldCom Inc. and Qwest Communications International Inc. Other stories involving accounting misdeeds, which had been in the background of the news for years, became front-page newspaper reports and feature stories on broadcast and cable television shows. Companies included household names such as AOL Time Warner Inc., Rite Aid Corp. and Xerox Corp.

Not coincidentally, two notable characteristics adorned each of the four massively scandal-ridden companies—Enron, Global Crossing, Qwest and WorldCom—that kept them out of the value investor's portfolio. First, they were all new, with WorldCom effecting an initial public offering in 1995, Global Crossing and Qwest both going public in 1997, and Enron revolutionizing during the mid-to-late 1990s from a stodgy natural gas company into a broadband and risk management outfit.

Second, these four companies (the "Big Four Frauds") stand out because their accounting aggressions took advantage of fantastic investor appetites. Attitudes subordinated the importance of balance sheet data, elevated appreciation for *pro forma* income reporting over GAAP-based earnings calculations and ignored the significance of depreciation exercises as proxies for required reinvestment. Corporate governance failures these companies epitomize reflected the investment population's simple indulgence of believing in fairy tales. Table 9.1 summarizes.

The multibillion dollar scale of the Big Four Frauds wrought proportional personal losses for millions of ordinary Americans. All this happened in the wake of the imploding financial bubble that stripped several trillion dollars from nonvalue investors, a large percentage from the same ordinary Americans.

Among nonvalue investors this combination of forces produced a natural tendency to overreact. The upshot was the wholesale questioning of the quality of financial reporting throughout corporate America. These calls were made worldwide.

Table 9.1 Antitheses of Value Investing

	ALL WERE NEW	SYMPTOMATIC AGGRESSION
Enron	1990s morphing	form over substance
Global Crossing	1997 IPO	*pro forma* devotion
Qwest	1997 IPO	reinvestment myopia
WorldCom	1995 IPO	balance sheet as hiding place

The Big Four Frauds of the late 1990s shared two singular characteristics: The companies were new, and all pursued aggressive accounting that reflected and exploited prevailing investor sentiment.

Perspective was required, but rarely broke through. Value investors classify the disparate scandals more clearly. They emphasize that Enron was essentially a Ponzi scheme, engineered and disguised by a coterie of "fiends" catering to a marketplace full of "investors" happy to play myopic marks in this game. They emphasize that the other three members—and many others—suffered from telecom mania on their way into the balloon, and telecom fever when it deflated.

More broadly, everyone should remember a self-evident fact: When the tech balloon held helium, few objected to manifestly aggressive accounting when business performance was measured by revenue, not earnings—eyeballs hitting Internet sites, not dollars customers paid. But victims do not like to be blamed.

ENRON: ACCOUNTING FORM OVER ECONOMIC SUBSTANCE

Enron through the 1980s was a natural gas drilling and pipeline company. It morphed through the financial boom of the late 1990s into a fiction trader booking false revenues. Its CEO, Kenneth Lay, was idolized by fans of management strategies fashioned in the heyday of that period's financial fantasies. In fact, he might have served as a fool while his lieutenants beguiled the business and investment communities.

Chapter 3 quotes the company's stated policy of making decisions based on reported accounting effects as opposed to underlying economic substance. Consider some consequences of this strategy.

The company engaged in thousands of transactions designed to house volatile trading activity in separate entities in order to insulate the company's earnings and hence stock price from the short-term gyrations attached to its trading activities. Using special-purpose entities is legitimate and lawful as matters of accounting and commercial and securities laws, so long as rules are observed.

To obtain off-balance-sheet treatment (discussed further in Chapter 11), the special-purpose entities must satisfy general well-known rules of consolidation accounting and particular arcane rules applied to these entities. The general rule provides that to avoid full consolidation of an entity, a third party must control a majority of that entity's equity; the arcane rule says that at least 3 percent of the total capital of the special-purpose entity must be equity (capping the debt-to-equity ratio at about 32:1).

In early transactions, Enron followed both rules, capitalizing SPEs with a debt-to-equity ratio no greater than 32:1 and placing a majority or all of the equity with a third party. In subsequent deals, however, one or both requirements went unmet, and in most of these either Enron, an affiliate, or an Enron executive held the equity. This meant that all the deals constituted related party transactions and all should have been consolidated on Enron's books. None was. The amount of debt housed in these controlled entities ran to billions of dollars, and the security was often Enron stock. When business conditions turned adverse, Enron's stock price weakened, and the debts came home to roost in cascades that led to bankruptcy.

Much of Enron's trading activity housed in the SPEs and much of its direct activity centered on the risk management business pursued through the development and trading of derivative securities. In this area, accounting rules call for real-time instrument valuation (called mark-to-market rules). The tendency was for Enron to use excessively rosy assumptions and aggressive allocation judgments—contrary to value investing's emphasis on accounting to reflect economic substance, not accounting to paint deceptively pretty pictures.

Managers assigned high asset values on exchanges and listed those amounts on the balance sheet and correspondingly high and theoretical profits in the income statement. In other cases, managers treated borrowed funds not as loans but as sale-and-purchase transactions—a modern version of a classic trick from the accounting fraud cookbook that value investors are alert to.

GLOBAL CROSSING: *PRO FORMA* FANTASIES AND CASH FLOW DREAMS

Global Crossing Ltd. was founded in 1997 by an executive with a checkered past who never ran a public company before. It described itself as providing telecommunications through an integrated global network reaching 27 countries and hundreds of major cities around the world. One goal was to lay cables under the Atlantic and the Pacific Oceans that would connect all the continents. This was the ultimate "story stock."

Nonvalue investors loved it. The company, incorporated in Bermuda, went public one year after its founding. It rapidly sported an insane market capitalization of nearly $40 billion. Two years later it was bankrupt amid evidence of accounting fraud.

As with its cohorts in the telecom industry, Global Crossing never had a serious business plan, steady CEO, or cash flows. As with many companies lacking such pillars of corporate sustenance and afflicted by anemic fundamentals, it stepped up its acquisition activity. It tried to buy growth to jump-start its stalled series of shaky business plans. Thanks to its insane market capitalization, it had a highly inflated currency to use in paying for acquisitions, which giddy sellers accepted with glee. Only nonvalue investors could have fallen into the trap of buying Global Crossing's stock.

Global Crossing was particularly adept at a form of financial felicity known as *pro forma* reporting, a technique used to conceal GAAP results. One of the most devastating accounting practices to have emerged amid tele-dot-com mania, *pro forma* accounting presents results by making a variety of non-GAAP entries. The result is a deliberate fiction.

The practice of *pro forma* reporting became so widespread during the 1990s that the difference between GAAP earnings per share (EPS) and *pro forma* EPS widened throughout the decade. The variance often produced reported results twice as good as GAAP results. The number of companies indulging the habit grew, extending beyond the tele-dot-com circus that popularized it. More than half those in the S&P 500 became hooked, though the tech industry led the way. Even after public outcry and legal crackdowns, many companies still report *pro forma* earnings.

This practice of ignoring rules that managers don't like is not limited to arcane esoteric accounting mysteries. Many companies preferred to report results under the *pro forma* rubric by ignoring such items GAAP considers expenses, such as sales commissions, marketing and personnel costs, and disbursements to start a new subsidiary. (No manager used the *pro forma* ruse to omit items of revenue such as sales, however.)

Global Crossing went to extremes, unmatched by more traditional companies and even those in its cohort, the leader in this charade among the Big Four Frauds. In August 2001, a finance executive discovered that the company and an Asian subsidiary had improperly reported *pro forma* values for cash revenue and adjusted cash flows based on measurements unrelated to usual accounting measures for cash receipts or earnings. He also expressed concern that cash amounts were inflated because they were based on transactions where either no cash was received or no monetary exchange occurred, but rather only exchanges of capacity occurred.

The company dismissed the warnings. It determined that its auditor had signed off on its annual reports that reflected the discrepancies. It noted that its public filings disclosed how the company determined the *pro forma* numbers, emphasizing that they should not be considered alternatives to GAAP figures. In those filings, the company said it used those figures to assess the performance and liquidity of its business segments.

The company also contended that it had disclosed its purchase of significant assets from carriers who were also customers, presenting the amounts of cash received and included in cash revenue and adjusted cash flows, as well as the amounts of the cash commitments it made.

Defending *pro forma* reporting by pointing to this disclosure is tantamount to admonishing users to ignore such a practice. But it is patently disingenuous. If investors are tacitly encouraged to pay *pro forma* figures no mind, then why is a company publishing them?

It's basically psychological manipulation. When earnings per share are reported on a *pro forma* basis at $3 whereas GAAP EPS is $1.50, you shouldn't tell a shareholder to ignore the $3 and focus on the $1.50. That is like trying to put toothpaste back in the tube.

An intelligent value investor isn't fooled by such sleight-of-hand use of *pro forma* figures. Value investors emphasize known, real results. They prefer hard data ascertained from the balance sheet. This is supplemented by facts drawn from the income statement concerning current earnings, adjusted by the analyst as necessary. Some attention may be paid to the cash flow statement to assess earnings quality or to examine factors relating to financial strength and business risk.

But value investing has no room for analysis based on *pro forma* data. Millions of nonvalue investors got this entire emphasis backwards. They put a premium on *pro forma* data and all but ignored the balance sheet.

QWEST: EXPLOITING MYOPIA REGARDING OWNER EARNINGS

Qwest Communications International Inc. was another newcomer to corporate America in the late 1990s. As with other telecoms, it suffered from excess investment in fiber optic cable. This put increasing pressure on its ability to generate sustained earnings and cash flows. For its part, Qwest teamed up with, among others, Global Crossing to create gimmick transactional accounting during the telecom boom.

Both provided local telephone services in the United States. A popular trick involved capacity swaps. The companies developed telecommunications capacity, incurring costs. Each then swapped that capacity with that from other telecom companies, including each other.

The pretext for capacity swaps between rival telecoms was to fill gaps in the other's networks. However, faulty bookkeeping recorded revenue based on the value of the swapped capacity. Costs were capitalized, allocated over numerous future periods.

To simplify for illustration, the company might incur $100 in costs to generate capacity another party would agree was worth $120 and get capacity worth $120 in return. The $120 is booked as revenue immediately, while the $100 in costs is spread over 5 years at $20 per year. Shazam.

The company got $120 in revenue with $20 in expense, for $100 in gross profit on the deal. Conservative accounting would have treated the swap as merely that, booking no revenue and could well have treated the entire $100 cost as an expense, contributing negative $100 to the bottom line. The difference between $100 to the good and $100 to the bad is night and day.

Even using less conservative accounting, the $100 in costs might be capitalized, producing a first year annual charge of only $20, but the difference between losing $20 and making $100 remains a difference between dusk and dawn.

These maneuvers concealed depreciation's role as a proxy of required reinvestment in the business (the core concept behind the idea of owner earnings discussed in Chapter 6). Cover was provided by investor appetite for cash flow analysis as opposed to examining the relationship between the balance sheet and the income statement, old-fashioned measures such as return on equity.

One pernicious characteristic of many accounting frauds is how easy it is to rationalize such moves. They often involve novel transactions, such as telecom capacity swaps, for which no direct authority exists. In their case, broadly applied conventional accounting principles would provide proper context.

Elementary accounting principles say that sales are recognized on the income statement when completed and expenses reliably contributing to future revenue generation capitalized. Drawing on those simple principles allows abusers to easily rationalize application to telecom capacity swaps. This was particularly true when nobody was looking, other than value investors who represented a distinct minority of the marketplace whose criticisms were disdained.

Determining how to account for novel transactions requires a dialogue between finance managers and their outside auditors. The conversation ordinarily involves the manager asking the auditor how the relevant industry treats such a transaction. The auditor usually reviews industry practice, whether prompted or not. The danger is that if the leading industry innovator is a fiend using aggressive accounting judgments, the consequent normal behavior is fiendish. The result is a contagion of accounting aggression.

Telecom capacity swaps were a case in point. They were an innovation of the telecom cohort that the industry began to adopt widely. The accounting developed uniformly, following the industry norms being ordained by the telecom members of the Big Four Frauds. The result was atrocious industrywide accounting.

The chosen accounting emphasized revenue as a central measure of financial performance, an orientation the era's nonvalue investors admired and widely rewarded. The contagion spread to other accounting areas where choices are permitted that affect revenue recognition. When one alternative produced higher revenue, it was selected.

However, accounting aggressions don't last. If you are realizing $100 of revenue this year against capitalized expenses of $20 to be taken annually over the next five, you need a similar amount of incremental revenue in those succeeding four years to run in place. (It is the Red Queen in Lewis Carroll's *Through the Looking Glass*, who had to keep running just to stay in the same place.) This might be doable for a while, but it is quite taxing. In the telecom industry of the latter

1990s, it meant doing more capacity swaps. But just as stamina constrains long-distance runners, new sources of phony accounting are finite. Value investors know this.

WORLDCOM: THE BALANCE SHEET AS A HIDING PLACE

WorldCom's fiasco typifies cases of fraudulent accounting that exploit an investment environment that paid too little attention to the balance sheet and too much attention to estimated cash flows extrapolated from an inflated income statement. As the nation's second-largest long-distance telecommunications carrier (marketed under the MCI brand), WorldCom's business was in tatters by 2000. The tech party wound down to its fateful fall. The telecom industry overspent, a downturn hit hard, and all players scrambled for business that wasn't there.

The company's habit of buying growth was thwarted when U.S. regulators rejected WorldCom's bid to buy Sprint Corp. With no new revenue streams and expenses mounting, WorldCom turned to accounting massage. The first push, in late 2000, was absorbing expenses by writing down various reserves on the balance sheet. That saved $1.2 billion in the last half of 2000. But more was needed. The company chose to shift expenses for line costs (amounts paid to local telecom networks to make connections) into asset accounts, boosting these to more than $4 billion in short order.

These tricks were uncovered by an internal spot check of the capital expenditure (cap-ex) records. Line costs would normally be characterized properly as routine business expenses, as the cost of generating current income. If so, such disbursements should have been recorded as current operating expenses. They should not have been capitalized (treated as assets to be written down over future periods).

The company's controller rationalized that these line charges would contribute reliably to future earnings, and there was some evidence that this belief was shared in the telecom community. But it did not jibe with GAAP. Several billion dollars of these disbursements were recorded in the cap-ex accounts, as assets on the balance sheet (not affecting the income statement), rather than in the expense accounts burdening net income.

As reported in 2001, line costs tallied about $15 billion, but should have been recorded at $22 billion. The result changed a year's worth of large losses into apparent paper profits for 2001 and 1Q 2002.

Amplifying the problem was the fact that in prior years line costs were expensed; the change to cap-exing them in 2001 thus also required some explanation.

Treating operating expenses as capital expenditures is an age-old move, and there is an age-old tendency for the abuser to overdo it, festooning the balance sheet with a bright red flag. A cap-ex account increasing by several billion dollars in a year stands out, even in a company of WorldCom's multibillion dollar size.

Value investing's interest in the balance sheet enabled the value investor to see WorldCom as a charade. Turning the balance sheet into a hiding place all but guaranteed the kinds of shenanigans the company practiced and for which nonvalue investors fell.

LOSERS AND WINNERS

What investment philosophies supported investing in the Big Four Frauds? Index funds were invested because these companies constituted slices of the broad market. Momentum investors drove much of the pricing mania associated with these companies, and reinforced managerial temptation to use accounting magic to drive inflated stock prices. Portfolio investors were attracted to any company whose stock price history measured by *beta* suited their risk appetites. Even growth investors participated, when they believed the stories of boundless growth ahead.

Only value investors stayed out. They did so by understanding the balance sheet's centrality, the importance of examining current earnings and making requisite adjustments to how they are reported. They understand the limits of cash flow analysis and the absurdity of *pro forma* reports. This is a powerful lesson about value investing's power and an explanation for why it fell from favor in the late 1990s and resurged in the early 2000s.

CHAPTER 10

CHRONIC REPORTING PROBLEMS

Value investing avoids frauds because it focuses on fundamentals, constantly alert for quirks that fraudsters use to conceal their handiwork. A deeper walk through the woods of accounting exposes a few accounting tricks long-used in financial reporting charades that likely would come to the attention of value investors doing business analysis.

REVENUE RECOGNITION

Revenue recognition refers to determining the top line on an income statement. Components of the exercise are the timing of recognizing a sale and the amount (as well as the risk that related invoices will not be paid and hence treated as an expense).

Enron violated revenue recognition principles when acting as broker between buyers and sellers of energy products. The fees it generated from this activity consisted of commissions calculated as a percentage of trade size. It treated as revenue not merely its relatively small percentage commission on the trade, but the entire amount of the traded contract, in aggregate. This violated the basic principle relating to the amount of a transaction recognized as revenue.

As for improper timing, Xerox is a good example. It entered into long-term lease agreements allowing lessees to use machines under contracts that required them to make periodic rental payments and sometimes giving an option to buy the machines. Proper revenue recognition would have recorded periodic rental payments as revenue when received. Instead, Xerox booked revenue when leases were signed, rather than over their life.

The McKesson-HBOC deal showcased violations of revenue recognition rules. The chief culprit was the booking of sales as final that in fact were contingent. The contingency related to side letters offering return privileges outside the company's ordinary sales practices. Some evidence showed more aggressive accounting practices, such as backdating sales contracts.

Another leading example is Sunbeam, maker of small appliances and camping gear. It shipped goods under contracts giving the buyer the right to return them. No sale was completed, yet the company treated the sale as closed, boosting revenue by recognizing it prematurely. Sunbeam also shipped out-of-season articles, such as charcoal grills, way ahead of demand, booking revenue for the transaction when shipped, rather than when customers ordered them later during grilling season.

EXPENSES: THE COSTS OF DOING BUSINESS

An elementary principle of accounting calls for matching items of expense with revenue. The effort devoted to running a business burdens income statements covering the periods when those efforts generate business results (that is, revenue). The amount, timing, and adjustment of expenses, therefore, adhere to principles akin to rules governing revenue recognition.

Most businesses sell some goods and services on credit and aren't going to receive payment for all the credit extended. From the company's viewpoint, amounts due from customers on credit sales produce accounts receivable. Typical accounts receivable call for payment within 30, 60, or 90 days, though some stretch out for 12 to 24 months or more.

Most companies selling on credit have a credit department that assesses customer credit quality and checks to assure that customers are current. When they're late, the company sends a dunning letter demanding payment. When that doesn't work after several tries, the company assumes the account won't ever be paid. Accounts deemed uncollectible become expenses, the cost of doing business giving credit.

Under the matching principle, the expenses are deemed to have occurred in the same period as the receivable was created and booked as revenue. This means every period managers must estimate what portion of revenue from receivables are going to become expenses. Managers never really know the right answer, but GAAP says to use history and err on the conservative side.

In estimating receivables charge-offs, it is difficult to be sure whether an estimate is too high or too low. It is also difficult to determine whether a previous estimate should be revised and reflected differently in succeeding periods. These decisions affect both the income statement and the balance sheet and do so for many periods. Gamesmanship is possible even in this most simple of accounting exercises. Value investors are aware of this play in the joints.

In the late 1990s, telecom equipment manufacturers sold to weak-credit businesses in the Internet sector whose overall prospects for repayment were dim. Yet the sales were recorded without adequately reserving for the likelihood that a good portion of the booked revenue would never translate into cash.

WorldCom was an abuser here as well. From 1998 through most of 2000, internal bookkeepers dutifully filed lists of deadbeat customers unlikely to pay their phone bills. Senior accounting officials routinely ignored these charge-off entries. Instead, they waited until the third quarter of 2000 and collected a large batch of receivables charge-offs together, aggregating $405 million. When that lump sum charge to earnings was recorded, it was presented and treated as a nonrecurring event. Value investors adjust current earnings when such large "one-time" charges appear (see Chapter 6).

For companies where receivables play a significant role or where the level of charge-offs is particularly significant in driving results—banks, consumer products businesses, and the like—value investors pay special attention to these line items on a balance sheet and the accompanying explanations concerning management policy.

Under the matching principle, the test for treating a disbursement as an expense today or one to be dribbled out over future time periods is whether the disbursement is likely to reliably contribute to earnings during those future periods. Disbursements not meeting that standard are matched to revenues generated currently, while those meeting that test are matched to revenues generated over those future periods.

The previous chapter's examples from the Big Four Frauds were not isolated cases. WorldCom's accounting for capacity swaps may be the most egregious, but its approach proliferated throughout the telecom and other boomerang industries during the late 1990s. They infected smaller outfits including Level 3 Communications and

360Networks, in addition to AOL Time Warner, all of which traded with both Qwest and Global Crossing.

Transactions included companies buying subscriber lines and network capacity in order to deliver content and service customers in exchange for the provider buying advertising in their media properties, print, broadcast, and online. No dollars changed hands, but each side determined that it generated revenue from the deal. Putting a value on such bartering deals is difficult, and the temptation is to inflate rather than understate the effect.

The capacity swap was also practiced in the energy and power trading industry during the late 1990s. But there a more streamlined version evolved that avoided the actual swapping. Companies engaged in "round-trip trades," purchase-and-sale transactions with the same counterparty at the same price for the same thing. The "round-trip" provided no economic benefit, was undetected or not prevented by internal controls and occurred at Enron and also apparently at Duke Energy and Reliant Resources Inc.

Capacity swaps and round-tripping are part of a broader category of barter trading that exploded during the "new economy" fad, where peddlers told investors to focus only on revenue growth, not expenses, profits, and sustainability. Value investors are not fooled by such fiction.

ACCOUNTING FOR DEALS

The shifting of expenses from current operations to capital expenditures can work in reverse. Enormous expenses are taken earlier in order to improve performance results later. This is a common scheme performed in connection with acquisition targets. If a business being bought can be stripped down by substantial expensing of assets, future expense recognition will be lower.

This scheme, sometimes referred to as a big bath, was a tactic routinely used by Tyco International Ltd., a company that closed hundreds of acquisitions in the few years of the boom. Part of this tactic, also allegedly performed by Tyco, is to treat as many disbursements as possible as costs of an acquisition rather than as ordinary operating costs. That both improves the target's apparent subsequent performance and reduces the apparent cost of operating the pre-acquisition business.

A topic of considerable debate in corporate America for the past few decades concerns accounting for a majority interest in another company. GAAP once permitted alternative approaches. If stock was the sole form of payment and other restrictions were met, deals could be treated as a business marriage, as a *pooling*. The assets and liabilities of the two companies were simply added together, with no up-front fuss or messy, ongoing adjustments.

Otherwise the deal was seen as a purchase and had to be treated like all purchases: The cost—the purchase price—is recorded on the buyer's balance sheet line by line based on what assets and liabilities were acquired. If, as is common, the price was greater than the line allocations, the excess was called "goodwill" (an accounting concept not to be confused with economic goodwill, a term used to designate a business bearing franchise characteristics). It would be treated like fixed assets, with a fraction of the total recorded as an expense in each year over several decades. This means annual expenses eating away at annual revenues, increasing managerial preference for pooling accounting.

Accounting rules that skew incentives toward one approach rather than another when the economic substance tells the manager to do something else leads to the kinds of accounting scandals seen every year. There are usually principled positions on each side, and the case of acquisition accounting is an example. Those favoring pooling pointed out that goodwill usually increases in value, so expensing it annually got things backwards. Those believing in purchase accounting pointed out that most deals involve a buyer and seller, not a marriage (merger) of equals, and accounting ought to be faithful to reality.

The sides recently compromised. The new rule says treat acquisitions as purchases, creating a goodwill account, but only expense that goodwill if it declines in value, not otherwise. As usually happens with compromises, this solves one problem—no skewed incentives toward meeting the pooling requirements—but opens up others. Who is to determine whether goodwill was impaired? It creates continuing opportunities for using the big bath and kindred techniques.

In fact, lots of goodwill write-downs occurred in the wake of this rule, many apparently products of funny business. The actions at AOL Time Warner received a fair amount of attention. The merger of those two companies was accounted for by creating a goodwill account. Subsequently the company's stock plummeted so severely that the accountants decided goodwill was impaired. The company took a charge of $54 billion, the largest in U.S. corporate history.

Value investors take moves like this seriously. The compromise rule on acquisition accounting creates enormous managerial discretion to determine if, when, and by how much, a write down of goodwill should be made. Management should explain decisions fully in annual reports. Disclosure should inform investors about the valuation effects of such events. Studying reports will show management's inclination toward using accounting to faithfully report underlying economics versus cosmetics.

THE CHALLENGE OF INTANGIBLES

Always valuable and always presenting tricky accounting questions, patents, trademarks, copyrights, and other intangible assets have gained business significance and accounting prominence. Some ins and outs are tricky enough to invite game playing by unscrupulous managers.

The basic idea is that if you develop and market it yourself, you record your expenses and leave it at that. When you buy it, you record the cost on the balance sheet. Whether it gets amortized is determined the same way the question is solved for goodwill: Its value is tested annually and if impaired it gets written off, otherwise it is left alone. The theory is also the same—most intangible assets neither decline in value nor wear out and don't require maintenance reinvestment. Intangibles that are impaired are written down accordingly.

There's also an exception for intangibles with fixed lives, like patents that expire after 17 years; this must be written off regularly over that lifetime. GAAP also requires disclosure about intangibles and their accounting treatment. Often this makes for interesting reading for companies possessing significant value stored in intangible assets. The disclosure says how the assets are classified, valued, and amortized, including estimates about useful lives.

None of this is perfect, making reading the narrative essential. Imprecision is why pure value investors hesitate to rely upon direct intangible asset values, but seek intangibles that create competitive advantages and barriers to entry. These values are signified by high and sustainable returns on equity.

SOURCES OF ILLUMINATION

Four important sources within an annual report reveal useful information concerning the corporation's culture manifested in its approach to accounting, whether about revenue recognition, goodwill impairment, or other accounting matters. See Table 10.1.

The most difficult raw source is numerical data. These are often products of choices GAAP permits, and the data are aggregated. While the limits of GAAP's choices and the data aggregation enable users to conduct financial analysis and valuation exercises, the formal and summary character of the data make it hard to glean from them special insights concerning managerial attitudes towards accounting and reporting frankness.

The second source is footnote disclosure accompanying the financial statements. These clarify the GAAP choices made, can illuminate the substantive meaning of the figures, and yield clues into the corporation's attitudes towards accounting. Chiefly this would consist of whether there is a tendency to prefer aggressive or conservative accounting treatments when choices are possible. Still, the formal character of this part of financial statements limits its transparency.

Better than the financials themselves is the narrative portion of annual reports called management's discussion and analysis (sometimes referred to as "MD&A"). This is intended to furnish an insider's interpretation of the figures. It should also provide readers with substantive understanding. To the extent MD&A does or does not succeed, this provides clues to managerial attitudes towards performance, how it is measured, and how important management believes conveying an understanding is.

The least formal and therefore best resource for assessing corporate culture and attitudes towards accounting are the letters executives write to shareholders in their annual reports. This vehicle is the least

Table 10.1 Disclosure: Sources and Quality

NUMERICAL	NOTES	MD&A	LETTERS
GAAP permits choices, ranging from aggressive to conservative, and data are aggregated	Formal explanations driven by accounting conventions can be difficult to penetrate independent of business simplicity and managerial candor	Insider's analytical view should provide more direct explanation but can remain dense	Top executives have opportunity for informal explanation with wide latitude revealing their capability and frankness

formal of the four chief sources of illumination. Chairmen and CEOs can tell it like it is, or at least how they see it. If reading these suggests a manager does not exploit this unique communication opportunity, value investors see this as a cautionary flag about the individual's sense of obligation and thus a negative reflection of the corporate culture and attitude toward accounting in the organization.

CHAPTER 11

FUTURE REPORTING PROBLEMS

Accounting games are as old as accounting. What changes is the favorite vases managers use. Currently important are the maneuvers catalogued in this chapter, areas of likely future exploitation against those investors who remain oblivious to the fundamentals of value investing that require examining and adjusting reported figures.

DERIVATIVES

Information not appearing in financial statements is easier to manipulate than that presented there. Taking the cake are derivatives, specialized financial instruments intended to hedge risks by laying off one risk against another (so that the position's value is *derived* from the relationship).

Suppose you owe interest on your mortgage at a fixed rate, but prevailing interest rates are lower and you predict they're likely to remain or go lower. You'd very likely join the millions of similarly situated people and refinance the mortgage. If you had to pay a penalty for doing so, you might try to find another way to achieve like results.

Suppose your brother has a floating-rate mortgage and a different view of the direction of future interest rates. He might be willing to agree to pay your mortgage for you at fixed rates in exchange for your payment of his mortgage for him at floating rates.

Companies swap interest rate payment streams like this routinely, with the swap's value derived from the relationship between rates. They also swap obligations relating to a range of benchmarks for which appetites differ. These include currency exchanges, the price of oil and other commodities, and infinite other matters, including the weather.

Measuring and recording derivatives are notoriously difficult accounting feats. In fact, they are so complex to account for that FASB took more than a decade to develop and enact applicable standards. For many years, as the market for these derivatives blossomed into a trillion-dollar business, they were not accounted for at all.

To see the difficulty, consider that in your brother-mortgage swap there is no doubt that each party believes it has struck value in the exchange. One is likely to be right and the other wrong, and that position may alternate as the years roll along. If rates stay low and go lower, you will be ahead; if the reverse happens, you will be on the losing end.

In some periods, you will rightfully declare you have saved money, and it would be reasonable to characterize it as having generated some form of revenue, or at least, avoided some expense. In those periods your brother will have incurred a loss or at least greater expense.

Whether from this brotherly swap you are saving or costing yourself money can be extended out through the mortgage's end, which might be as long as 30 years. Estimating the value of either is fiendishly difficult, calling for vast judgment. Companies face similarly daunting tasks in sizing up derivatives positions.

Accounting rules finally enacted in the late 1990s call for measuring derivatives at fair value and recording them in the balance sheet as assets or liabilities. But fair value can change daily, and there's not always a reliable market to measure it. Estimates are necessary. They are particularly difficult to make in the case of derivatives because of the limited historical track record. This makes applying fundamental principles such as conservatism more difficult than in conventional contexts. Consequently, the exercise is especially prone to extremes of aggressive and fraudulent.

GAAP rules on derivatives are intricate in proportion to the instruments themselves and can't detain us here. Useful to know is that current rules require extensive discussion of how a company uses them and how they account for them. Value investing calls for studying these explanations. Doing so promotes understanding of how management thinks about business and accounting and whether investors should want to take an equity stake.

OFF-BALANCE-SHEET TRICKS

Runner-up for pretending-it's-not-there accounting is the gambit of off-balance-sheet financing, one of a few accounting issues Congress addressed directly in the Sarbanes-Oxley Act responding to the Big Four Frauds of the late 1990s. Enron used thousands of special purpose entities to house debt whose proceeds corporate headquarters used but that did not burden the performance report card. Many entities were managed by Enron executives, making negotiations easy and creating a network of conflicts of interest.

It became clear in late 2001 that Enron had failed during the preceding four years to make proper disclosure concerning these "related-party transactions" that were designed to be treated as "off-balance-sheet" transactions. In a flagrant but not atypical case, Enron held an investment in a Polish company it couldn't sell, so it sold it to one of these friendly partnerships, booking a "profit." The profit showed up in the income statement, but details were not disclosed.

The initial consequences were staggering and only worsened. Twenty percent of Enron's shareholders' equity was wiped out—a total of $2.2 billion. The company restated its financials for the preceding four years, producing a 20-percent reduction to reported cumulative net income of nearly $600 million ($96 million in 1997, $113 million in 1998, $250 million in 1999 and $132 million in 2000). On the balance sheet, consolidation increased debt by approximately $628 million in 2000 and like amounts in earlier years.

GAAP requires related-party transactions such as these to be disclosed. They call for describing the relationship of the parties, the types and dollar amounts of deals, and their effect on the financial statements. Discussion must include how terms were reached, how methods changed over time, and critically, cannot hint that arms'-length terms were reached without substantiating the claim. Enron gave brief and vague waves at these rules, revealing the existence but no details of the arrangements.

The rules relating to the "off-balance-sheet" portion of the Enron escapades are more subtle. Equity investments (below 20-percent voting power) are shown on the balance sheet at *fair value*, with gains, losses, and dividends generally allocated to income accounts. Medium stakes (20 percent to 50 percent) are reported at cost then adjusted each year to reflect changes in the owners' equity of the investee, based on its earnings or losses, with cash dividends seen as a conversion of equity into cash. Ownership of 50 percent or more voting power carries control rights and calls for accounting on a consolidated basis, meaning all assets and liabilities of the sub being put on the parent's books, less any minority interest held by others.

These rules tempt managers to exploit the seemingly bright line between the equity and consolidation methods set at the 50-percent ownership level. For example, why not negotiate investments in investees at exactly 49.5 percent rather than greater? That means a single line item on the investor's balance sheet showing "equity investments" at adjusted cost, not full inclusion on the parent's financials of all line items of the subsidiary, including debt. This is the core of "off-balance sheet-financing"—getting assets to work for you without having to show them and related costs on your report card.

As with other accounting manipulations, off-balance-sheet financing makes the value investor's work more difficult. It requires making adjustments to the balance sheet and income statement to address hidden burdens and costs. The best strategy for dealing with this obfuscation is simply to avoid investment targets whose managers report financial data in ways that suggest opacity or undue complexity.

PENSIONS

Pension funds can be mischief grounds for bad accounting too. These are funds managed on behalf of employees. Funds are invested in securities so that the account value rises and falls with investment results. Also fluctuating are the probable payouts, as employees retire and die and expectations about when those events happen change. Measuring investment value and probable liability claims require making judgments.

Fund managers have to estimate rates of return on invested assets, for example, as well as make actuarial guesses about the aging of the workforce and mortality rates. These guesses can produce situations where assets exceed liabilities or the reverse. For the company, that means gains or burdens, and the result gets picked up on the company's own financial statements. The rules, as usual, are intricate, but there is an important one value investors emphasize.

GAAP permits companies to treat pension benefit costs as expenses and pension asset income as revenue. In each case, moreover, GAAP permits using estimates of expected annual return on pension assets as the measure of income even if not earned. Optimistic estimates equate to unfounded earnings.

It is not uncommon to see estimates of 10-percent annual gains, although long-run average U.S. returns on equity range around 7-8 percent. This simple figure, easy to ascertain, is a quick screening device to eliminate investment targets as unsuitable for value investors. Any company using more than 9 or 10 percent can be excluded automatically, unless special circumstances justify and other factors point in the opposite direction.

STOCK OPTIONS: A CASE OF NONACCOUNTING

Winner of the no-accounting prize is stock options. These devices skyrocketed during the 1990s to form a large compensation pool at many companies. Stock options typically give the right to buy stock during a specified period for a specified price. Typically the price is at or higher than the prevailing stock price when the option is issued. The goal is to create incentives for recipients to manage the company well—doing so boosts earnings and, in turn, stock price, generating higher compensation.

For political reasons, GAAP never summoned the courage to compel treating these things as expenses on an income statement. No doubt payments to employees in cash are expenses. And no doubt payments in stock are as well. The standard argument against expensing options is they are hard to value. But this defense is a charade because (a) developed methods and markets are available to aid valuation and (b) while using these is difficult, it is no more so than many other exercises in accounting and business valuation. Politics and power are the reasons, and one bright side of the Big Four Frauds is movement towards a practice of expensing them.

One dark side, however, is the lack of political will in Congress to formally require doing so. While members of Congress discussed it, they backed off when push came to shove. No good reason except politics explains this retreat either, for many other provisions of the law Congress passed in response to the Big Four Frauds invade the province of other regulators better suited to the task.

Politics did not prevent FASB from requiring significant disclosure concerning stock-option awards. It even requires companies to disclose the "as if" effects on net income and earnings per share of stock options outstanding. This is crucial data for value investing that corporate leaders who support proper stock option accounting are putting directly on the income statement. Soon it might be unnecessary to dig into the footnotes. But value investors are cautious with companies unwilling to say on the first page what stock options cost owners.

A compromise amid the politics enabled another accounting rule to pass, concerning *variable option plans* (generally those where the exercise price or other terms could vary depending on subsequent events). The requirement catches stock option repricing strategies. This occurs when previously granted options fail to do their work and the stock price falls below the exercise price rather than soars above.

The move lowers the price, reintroducing the same incentive that didn't work on the previous grant. (Handball players will recognize this as akin to a "do-over.") GAAP says that kind of action is a recordable cost. There's an easy way around this one, however, which is to cancel the previous plan, wait a respectable period of time, and issue a new one. That gets the manager back into the *la la land* of no accounting for stock options.

Value investors might disagree with each other on accounting policy. For example, value investors hold different views about how to account for stock options (in addition to whether they should be used at all). The key thing they look for is managerial discussion of the reasons for using stock option compensation and the reasons for choosing to account for them in a particular way. Disclosure quality can be as strong an indication of managerial ability and integrity as can their sparing use and most conservative accounting. Value investors judge for themselves.

CHAPTER 12

WAYS TO BUY EQUITIES

Value investing requires hard work. Is it worth one's time to do detailed analysis of business? Why not just let others do the work and then take advantage of their effort?

That is the recipe for herd behavior at the core of market gyration. You join the boom-to-gloom crowd and ride the euphonic wave up and suffer the depressing drop down. It is much safer, socially and psychologically speaking, to do that. We're all in that together and misery loves company. This explains the attractiveness of all forms of nonvalue investing.

But the herd strategy is far less financially enriching, a fact of economic history. It is why value investors are more successful, despite attracting a smaller following. Despite the small following, on the other hand, traits intuitive to value investors are also inherent in all forms of investing, whether conscious or not, and apply to every investment vehicle used to buy equities. These traits and their universal application form part of what value investing is. Value investing is investing.

For equities, value investing seeks to find those determined by valuation analysis to be the cheapest, to offer the largest margin of safety. The apparent thriftiness in this position bears emphasis. Value investors minimize costs of investment. These include the costs of trading, commissions, and taxes. While value investing does not prescribe allowing these to drive an investment selection, it does include these costs in assessing returns and therefore preferences.

INDEX FUNDS AND VALUE INVESTING

What does value investing have in common with long-term investment in an index fund? While it appears that index funds relieve an investor of the difficulties of value investing, this view is somewhat misleading.

Index funds are mutual funds whose managers allocate capital by buying all stocks of a particular description, usually all stocks comprising a broad market segment as indexed by some benchmarking firm such as Standard & Poor's, keepers of the S&P 500.

These managers choose which of many possible indexes to mimic, ranging from the S&P 500 (larger companies), to the Russell 2000 (smaller companies), Wilshire 5000 (a large mix of different sorts of companies), and others. Under relentless competition for capital to invest, index fund managers often boast that their index outperforms the next guy's index. People opting for index funds know their limits and realize they can't outperform the market, whether due to lack of time, insight, money, or what have you.

Index funds work especially well during booms. They look wretched amid busts. Buying a slice of a rising market makes you look smart and feel rich. Owning it during the fall feels intellectually weak and financially suicidal. Index funds grew during the boom and have deflated during the bust. Still they might be the best way to go, for those unable to distinguish wheat from chaff or economic reality from popular belief.

Investing in stocks remains a risky business, whether you own a share of stock or an indexed market slice. Value investing is unavoidable, even for an indexer: it still requires at least some marginal basis for believing value is greater than price. There is no shortcut in the business of investing.

Common sense and experience tell this much. Passive investor is a contradiction in terms. That goes for ownership of businesses such as Ford or ExxonMobil as much as it does for the funds of Vanguard or Fidelity. Single shares move and so do markets. Both go up and both go down. Bear markets often last for years, sometimes decades.

EQUITY FUNDS

Equity funds can also be run by professional stock pickers. Investors take a stake and pay a fee for the pros, making the approach more costly than index funds. In advertising, this fee is more than offset by performance, though in reality this is often not the case. The stock picking includes buying as well as selling, and therefore also carries tax consequences for investors. The stock picker controls these, not investors.

Some mutual funds are closed-end, meaning to buy into one you have to buy from an existing shareholder, usually in an open-market-exchange transaction. More numerous are open-ended funds, where anyone can buy in or cash out at any time directly through the fund. Either type gives an investor professional management, for a fee, and the opportunity to diversify, at a potential cost.

Again, there is no rocking-chair solution to investing. In the end, all styles of investing—indexing, technical, growth, or portfolio—implicate value. What distinguishes value investors is an up-front willingness to engage in the requisite mental exercises.

DRIPS

To control tax consequences from equity investing, individual stocks can be bought and sold. Dividend reinvestment plans (DRIPs) are an attractive method. These are often programs run commission-free by individual companies, enabling investors to regularly reinvest dividend payments in new shares and to increase holdings.

DRIPs are useful to impose self-discipline for those otherwise easily distracted from adding principal to their investment resources—not a value investing trait but DRIPs can be attractive to value investors for their convenience. Dividends paid on account shares are automatically reinvested when declared, rather than paid to the holder.

For regular dividend-paying companies, this can mean steady additions to equity securities. DRIPs also typically offer holders the chance to have funds automatically taken from bank accounts at designated times to buy additional shares. Investors can set dates to follow paydays, creating additional discipline that yields substantial sums.

A key benefit of the steadiness of DRIP funding is that dollars are invested at regular intervals, when price is below value and when above. If maintained over a long period, these discrepancies result in owning shares purchased at an average cost lower than the average of the prices on each purchase date. Hence the term "dollar cost averaging."

While certainly not pure value investing, DRIP's dollar-cost-averaging can produce impressive investing gains. And there are value investing attributes of using DRIPs. DRIPs and dollar cost averaging reduce the number of decisions an investor must make. They are also attractive because few stocks meet properly defined value investing criteria. Value investors monitor the fundamentals of the businesses and only take action to stop buying or to sell when preset fundamental factors have deteriorated to preset levels.

EXCHANGE-TRADED FUNDS

Cross-fertilizing in financial markets and products accelerates. One result is the exchange traded fund (ETF). This is a cross between securities and mutual funds begun in 1993 and now boasting more than 100 offerings. These ETFs grew in popularity during the tech boom, with enormous flows of capital being sent to the QQQ, the ticker symbol for the Nasdaq 100 ETF.

ETFs are akin to open-ended mutual funds in that both pool contributed investor capital to buy and sell a range of securities, with fund valuation based on the portfolio's net asset value, and with unlimited new shares issuable. ETFs are akin to stocks and closed-end mutual funds in that they are repriced constantly during every trading day (open-ended mutual fund shares are priced and can be bought and sold only once a day, at the net asset value determined at the market's close).

Securities in ETFs are typically based on an index, not managerial stock picking. The Nasdaq 100's QQQ is an example. It is comprised of positions in each of the 100 companies designated as constituting that index. Other examples are the iShares series offered by Barclays Global Investors and the S&P 500 product called SPDRs (marketed by State Street Global Advisors). ETFs also basket the Dow, as well as smaller market niches such as small-cap or emerging market. Bond ETFs are rising in popularity, with some focusing on corporate bonds and others on government issues.

Periodic costs to investors in ETFs are usually lower compared to mutual funds that pay managers substantial sums for their stock-picking prowess. Without that cost, fees tend to be more in line with index funds. Some ETFs are even cheaper than index funds, because the back office work is conducted by brokers who do the buying and selling rather than by the fund itself. But brokers don't work for free, so trading costs can erase the savings on periodic costs. The upshot: One-time large investments profit from using the ETF structure (an up-front broker fee but lower annual fees) whereas dollar-cost average investing profits from the mutual fund route (higher annuals but no broker fees).

HEDGE FUNDS

Possibly coming soon to some retail brokerages are hedge funds, the financial services innovation that until the mid-2000s was the preserve of the superrich. If they follow the path of other investment vehicles towards the end of the twentieth century, these outlets may proliferate. The key activity is a combination of buying securities outright and capping both the upside and the downside, using a mix of call and put options.

Hedging refers to a practice of taking investment positions that limit the downside and cap the upside potential. Suppose that Microsoft's common stock is trading on February 3 at $23.70 per share. A *mutual fund manager* buys a large number of shares of Microsoft common at that price. A *hedge fund manager* buys some Microsoft calls and "writes" (sells) others. Say he buys those denominated as "Microsoft $22.50 calls at $3.20" (the $22.50 defines the strike price and the $3.20 is the cost) and writes those denominated as "Microsoft July $32.50 calls at $0.25." Each expires July 20.

Suppose on July 20, Microsoft common is trading at $40 per share. If the mutual fund manager sells the stock, she gains $16.30 per share. That is, she gains $40 – $23.70 per share. If the hedge fund manager and his counterparty both exercise their options, he gains $7.05 per share. That is, he buys at $22.50 and sells at $32.50, yielding a $10 per share gain. Then subtract the $3.20 paid for the call option and add the $0.25 earned on writing the call.

Suppose instead that on July 20 Microsoft common is trading at $15 per share. If the mutual fund manager sells the stock, she loses $8.70 per share. That is, she loses $23.70 – $15. The hedge fund manager loses $2.95 per share. Both options are out-of-the-money and the net option cost is $2.95 ($3.20 minus .25).

Accordingly, while the long position offers greater upside (a gain of $16.30), it also exposes greater downside (a loss of $8.70). The hedged position collars the range in both directions (capping the gain at $7.05 but also limiting the loss to $2.95).

Hedge fund managers sometimes designate themselves as adopting particular investing styles, including that of value investing. This label is potentially misleading. A fund may engage in the sort of fundamental valuation analysis value investors conduct. But value investing is more than fundamental analysis. Its risk-hedging strategies are principles such as the circle of competence and especially the margin of safety, not calls and puts.

The tools hedge funds use are less akin to the margin of safety than to the theory of risk associated with modern finance theory measured by *beta*. Hedging with options appears directed toward minimizing risk of price volatility, not investment and valuation judgment. Value investors will be aware of this distinction if and when hedge funds become more widely available to the general investing public.

A final point to make about hedge funds: There is often more in the label than in the practice. Many hedge funds practice no hedging at all. Instead, they buy and sell securities in the same way any ordinary mutual fund does. The chief difference seems to be that under our securities laws, mutual funds are heavily regulated as "investment companies," whereas hedge funds avoid this regulation. If the mutual fund scandals of the early 2000s caused a major stir in investment circles, watch out for a likely scandal involving hedge funds in the mid-to-late 2000s.

ALTERNATIVES TO EQUITIES

Value investors habitually relate price to value. This attitude applies not only to equities, but also to all other investments. The habit of relating price and value comes more naturally for certain assets than others. Real estate is a good example. People seem intuitively able to understand that they might be getting a "good deal" on real estate, but many exhibit less intuition when thinking about common stock investments. They do likewise with consumption goods such as cars and loans or leases taken to finance their purchase.

Markets for some alternatives show how price-value differences are less likely to appear. Bonds are a good example. These instruments have features such as duration and interest rate that common stocks lack. This makes it easier for investors to agree on their value and produces prices more reflective of value. The absence of these features on common stocks suggests reasons to believe that price-value differences are likely to occur on common stocks.

So alternatives to equities both illustrate the universality of value investing principles and reinforce the key element of relating price to value. This justifies summarizing some alternatives to equities.

BONDS

For any given company, bonds are safer compared to stocks. Whereas stocks promise nothing and come last in bankruptcy, bonds are senior in bankruptcy, offer a designated return, and come with covenants furnishing additional protection. Bonds are an investment in a particular issuer, however, and the same valuation and analysis rules apply to both: Stick with high-quality companies within one's circle of competence and run by trustworthy, capable managers.

Bonds are IOUs. The issuer promises to repay the borrowed amount (principal), along with periodic interest payments. The covenants require maintaining various financial cushions to assure payment on the bonds, restrict the issuer's right to disburse cash for uses that would impair its ability to repay the bonds, and specify the relative seniority of the bonds in case the issuer becomes insolvent or bankrupt.

Public bonds are listed on a secondary market, such as the New York Stock Exchange, where investors trade them. They are issued through prospectuses containing detailed information about the issuer's business and the particular features of the bonds. Issuers file periodic reports with the SEC and rating agencies such as Standard & Poor's, Moody's, and Fitch that prepare frequent analyses of bond credit quality.

Global credit conditions and the issuer's creditworthiness determine the price–the interest rate–on debt. Applying general principles of asset valuation, the value of a bond is the present value of its future cash flows. These are (1) the periodic interest payments plus (2) the principal to be repaid at maturity. The rate used to compute these values is a rate that gives an acceptable rate of return, reflecting the issuer's credit risk and prevailing credit market conditions.

Bond values change as the issuer's creditworthiness changes and as credit markets fluctuate. In general, during booming stock markets, bonds are priced low compared to equity, but pay a regular return. During stock market busts, bonds face less downside risk than comparable equities.

When an issuer's creditworthiness declines (say its debt:equity ratio rises substantially or its liquidity is impaired) or the credit market becomes pessimistic about finance (interest rates rise), higher discount rates are necessary to value the bond's cash flows. As the issuer's creditworthiness or market conditions improve, lower rates apply.

Either way, the face value of the bond differs from the present value of its cash flows. The difference is either a premium (when the bond sells for more than face value) or a discount (when the bond sells for less than face value).

As the market value of the bond changes, reflecting interest rate fluctuations, the yield to bondholders changes. The return to bondholders is called the "effective yield" or "market rate." For bonds selling at a discount, the effective yield is higher than the coupon. For bonds trading at a premium, the effective yield is lower than the coupon.

These relationships reflect the inverse relationship between the value of a bond and prevailing market interest rates. As interest rates rise, the value of bonds outstanding falls and vice versa. Consider a bond with a coupon of 10 percent. If market rates fall to 5 percent, that bond is worth more than newly issued bonds (better to get 10 percent than 5 percent after all); if rates rise to 15 percent, it is worth less (you can get superior returns investing in newly issued bonds). One insight: Buying bonds is particularly productive when interest rates are high compared to historical averages—they are more likely to fall than they otherwise would.

Bond analysts tend to be more objective than their equity counterparts. Credit rating agencies devote tremendous analytical firepower to grading bonds and have no interest in buying or selling them. (Major investment banking firms analyze equities, but other parts of the same firms trade them.)

Other investors, particularly institutional investors, do the same homework as the rating agencies. That usually means that when a credit rating agency issues a downgrade, it follows previous downward pressure on the price and creates more. The double effect often overdoes it, making post-downgrade bond purchases possible value opportunities. The cognate: Upgrades mean a price probably higher than justified.

Bonds pay no more than they promise, of course, whereas equity owners enjoy their slice of an enlarging pie when corporate performance is strong. One way to hedge a bet is to buy a hybrid, convertible bonds.

CONVERTIBLES

Convertible bonds give investors the relative safety of a bond with the potential upside of stock. The fixed-income feature of bonds helps investors ride through market downturns. The convertible feature gives upside potential. The combination means that the bond component is relatively easy to value and is likely to be priced accordingly; the equity value component is more variable and opens up possibilities for disagreement and price-value discrepancies.

There is always a price to pay for safety, of course, and the convertible bond is no exception. The price in the case of convertible bonds is about 1/3 in forgone upside when the equivalent equity performs well. The benefit is that they cost only about 2/3 the downside of equity when things go poorly. The difference in the cost-benefit matrix is due to the cushion delivered by fixed interest and principal payments, while straight equity holders amid adversity might get nothing.

Bonds produce a higher return measured by liquidity, on average, because interest yields on debt for typical issuers are higher than dividend yields on common stock. The spread widens for more aggressive or optimistic companies. These plow back all or most of net income. They calculate that doing so will boost income further, followed by a rising stock price that will make converting the debt to equity appealing.

For straight debt, credit rating agency grades are probably more important and accurate than for convertibles. Raters dominantly test for credit quality measured by the issuer's ability to pay its debts as they come due. They do the same thing for convertibles, effectively giving no value to the equity feature that can pay handsomely.

The convertible bond market tends to be less efficient than either the stock or straight bond markets, making the prospects for finding convertible bonds priced differently than value greater. As an asset class, convertible bonds are attractive in any market environment, from boom to bust. They are safe on the way up through enjoying the ride and on the way down through a landing that bottoms out on the principal and interest, far above the deep bottom (zero) stockholders face.

Convertibles might be best suited for those facing a shorter time horizon, say only a few years from retirement or needing resources for other specific needs. Another trade-off: Exploiting convertible bonds calls for a somewhat more hands-on approach than with straight equity because the conversion feature can trigger redemption by the issuer and usually expires on a designated date. When conversion value exceeds the bond's debt value, the holder might need to make a conversion election within a short time frame.

REAL ESTATE

Most people purchasing real estate seem to believe it is possible to get a "good deal." By this they embrace the possibility that price and value are different things, suggesting that when it comes to home ownership, people intuit the core quality of value investors.

Home ownership in the United States has risen steadily, fueled by federal support for the trading of mortgages in secondary markets. It also reflects the U.S. tax code's deductibility of mortgage interest on primary homes and real estate taxes. By staking a modest down payment (often 10 to 20 percent), much of the population exploits the leverage afforded by putting more assets to work for them.

Except for speculative fever in select times and places, real property values rise reliably, making such an investment a reasonable vehicle to increase net worth. Americans have been able to tap the increased equity value in primary residences in recent decades by using home equity vehicles dotting the market. Low-interest-rate-environments spur refinancing transactions that, by lowering debt service obligations, free up cash flow as well.

Buying secondary homes for use as vacation getaways or rental properties has also become more attractive to many American families, no longer the preserve of the upper echelons. Particularly in periods of low interest rates and sagging stock market returns, these markets offer attractive value investments.

Apart from the additional concerns of family needs and psychic rewards, the basic principles of valuation apply to these vehicles. Paying a price reasonably below estimated value remains important. Avoiding excessive leverage is akin to avoiding margin trading on equities. Patience is likewise valuable.

Another advantage to home ownership is that the owner is the manager—he runs the home, maintains it, determines required reinvestment to maintain and improve its value, and so on. Value-minded investors are sure they can do these tasks, or else turn the reigns over to someone who can. These points go doubly for vacation or rental properties that might present logistical problems.

An increasingly accessible vehicle that spurts real estate investment and gained enormous popularity throughout the 1990s is the real estate investment trust (REIT). REITs are pooled investments that issue debt or equity to investors and use the proceeds to acquire and hold real estate interests. A REIT may focus on particular projects, such as office parks or apartment buildings, or regions, such as the southeastern or northeastern United States, or both.

A REIT's value is affected by changes in the value of the properties or loans it holds. It depends on the cash flows from those assets to repay its investors. The upside and downside of REITs are tied to those of real property held directly. The benefit is ease of acquisition, small minimum investment required, and built-in diversification. There are also appealing tax advantages. The same value-investing mind-set, comparing price with value, applies to these investments.

INTELLECTUAL PROPERTY

All investors know about the rising importance of intellectual property, which drives business value. Patents, trademarks, copyrights, and other assets lacking physical characteristics can generate cash flows dwarfing those generated by traditional "hard" assets such as property, plant, equipment, and machinery.

Less well considered are the prospects for owning these devices. Authors and songwriters are entitled to copyrights, inventors to patents. These rights rarely generate huge income for innovators, but creators don't ignore them.

Investors can buy an interest. Those who want to own royalties to the entire fabled output of British rock star David Bowie, for example, look no further than the asset securitization deal he did. Effected in February 1997, the deal raised $55 million based on the rights to 250 songs, a 15-year maturity and boasted a coupon of 7.9 percent. It was the first securitization of privately held intellectual property rights and the first for music recording rights.

Securitization deals are time-tested vehicles to pool varied assets, including all types of intellectual property, and issue securities backed by their cash flows. The vehicle is a special trust whose sole assets are the property transferred to it. And backing the deal, in the Bowie case, was an assignment of the royalty stream on various recordings.

The trust is its own legal entity. It issues securities that typically trade on public capital markets. At this stage, the security is more like a bond than a stock, a claim to a fixed share of interest and piece of principal on the trust's asset. Excess amounts go to the artist.

The securities are fixed-income instruments, akin to bonds and exhibiting the same sort of price-value relationship. They typically are rated by one of the rating agencies, usually a high-grade rating such as A or better. Requisite credit quality for such a rating is sometimes achieved by a guarantee of the payment stream secured from a AAA-rated financial institution, or by creating a cash reserve in the trust from the artist's residual share to fund shortfalls.

A lot of cash flows through the stream, and it is important to understand who is entitled to what. Artists get paid only from royalties granted in their recording-company contracts. Only those assets support the trust, not the artist's other assets. Songwriters and publishers share in three types of royalties: publishing, broadcast performance, and synchronization (as in commercials). Publishers also enjoy mechanical royalties, what record companies pay to use original or cover versions of songs.

The Bowie deal is an example of individual music royalty securitization. Another form is bundling securitization, where royalties of multiple artists are combined into a pool. Bundling is favored by record companies who have under contract a number of solid artists who collectively support a deal, but individually could not.

Keep an eye for deals offered by a range of intellectual property holders in a variety of fields. To date, these include Motown denizens Edward Holland, Lamont Dozier and Brian Holland ("Stop! In the Name of Love"), James Brown, the Isley Brothers, Iron Maiden, and Rod Stewart.

Other assets being thrown into the mix are television syndications, including those of the hit *Seinfeld*. Also in the cards are literary writers such as Dr. Seuss, professional sports teams, and the contracts of individual athletes.

PRECIOUS METALS

Valuation of precious metals such as gold and silver differ from other investments. It is common to refer to the intrinsic value of a business, measurable from discounted future cash flows it stands to generate. The reference assumes a baseline of cash as a vehicle of value.

In times of extreme political and economic crisis, however, and at a deep level of mercantilism, paper values turn worthless and the store of value returns to precious metals. During such times, possessing a modicum of instruments carrying this deep intrinsic value might be prudent.

Silver is the economic preserve of last resort. When paper assets plummet amid calamitous world events, silver holds its own or better. (Gold will also skyrocket in price; see below.) A modicum of this metal deserves consideration for a small portion of every investor's portfolio (between a few and 10 percent, depending on market environments).

Silver is an investment, so the same rules apply. Value investors in silver understand how the metal is extracted, processed, used, and bought and sold. In short, they understand the effects of supply and demand on silver's value. Of more general significance, silver is an industrial metal, meaning there is substantial organic demand for it as a productive input.

On the supply side, for example, silver is often a by-product of copper, a base metal. Thus when copper prices rise, silver prices tend to fall. On the demand side, its leading use is in film (hence the silver screen). However, development and proliferation of digital imaging, which does not consume silver, reduces demand for the metal and puts downward pressure on its price.

The easiest way to buy silver is in bullion bars and small-denomination coins. These are usually fairly priced compared to value, and dealers also invariably charge some premium. Large markups destroy the value of commemorative and decorative silver coins and jewelry, making these vanity items rather than prime investment vehicles. Price and value of these instruments might vary because people form personal attachments that put private valuations above market valuations.

One way to tap into the silver investment market is through the shares of silver mining companies. Rising metal prices tend to help producers, but falling metal prices do not proportionately hurt. The performance and hence stock prices of mining companies can remain strong even when precious metals markets are weak. Valuations based on estimated company cash flows are a function of both earnings from current production and probable earnings arising from proven and probable reserves, an exception to pure value investing's usual aversion to estimating earnings growth.

Gold, while enjoying many industrial applications from electronics to chemistry, is mainly a monetary metal. Its value is a function more of macroeconomic forces, such as interest rates, currency fluctuations, and inflation levels. This makes it more sensitive than silver and other precious metals to surprising structural shocks. Examples range from the move away from the gold currency standard to gold divestiture by central banks. While gold once served as a definitive hedge against high inflation and interest rates, derivative financial products such as futures and options have replaced its leadership role.

COLLECTIBLES

Silver can be a straight investment or can assume the characteristic of collectibles. Rare silver coins or chalices, for example, can store value. The same is true for paintings, vintage posters, sculptures, and other *objet d'art*, as well as antiques such as watches, cars, and furniture.

These are often terrific investments measured in the total economic return generated. On the other hand, they invariably produce emotional attachments that can make parting with them difficult, even for substantial premiums.

Such collectibles when owned should certainly be seen as part of one's portfolio for purposes of assessing overall economic position, risk, and prospects. But appropriate discounting for the emotional side is required. It is far easier to sell a $1000 bank certificate of deposit or 100 shares of IBM in an emergency than to sell a dozen U.S. silver dollars. This again underscores the difference between price and value at the heart of value investing.

Table 13.1 summarizes the alternative investments and associated price-value relationships discussed in this chapter.

Table 13.1 Alternative Investments and Price-Value Relationships

Straight Bonds	Duration and coupon drive valuation and price
Convertible Bonds	Equity component drives variability, some price-value divide
Real Estate	Buyers intuit a price-value divide when seeking "good deals"
Precious Metals	Supply-demand imbalances drive price-value divide
Other Collectibles	Personal attachments drive price-value divide

CHAPTER 14

SUMMARY OF TENETS

Value investing is ultimately common sense applied to capital allocation. Its general philosophy and key tools summarized in previous chapters can be distilled further. Worth extracting are the following 10 value-investing tenets.

MR. MARKET PRINCIPLE

Value investors make a habit of relating price to value. They recognize that stock markets rise and fall. The prices of individual stocks likewise swing widely. In the case of stocks and stock markets, a bull exhibits excessive optimism, a bear excessive pessimism. Dreary rationality, where value investors live, lies in between. There are stocks priced above what the underlying business is really worth and stocks priced below that. While over long periods of time the process evens out, the ideal strategy is to search aggressively for investment prospects priced below value.

BUSINESS ANALYST PRINCIPLE

Value investors do not guess when the market or a stock is at its peak, trough, or specific points in between. There will nearly always be times when some positions are priced attractively compared to value and others when the opposite is the case. During periods characterized by bullishness, as the late 1990s, there are fewer value opportunities; during bearish times, as in the early and mid-2000s, there are more. The universe of prospects enlarges as markets fall and contracts as they rise. Tendencies in either direction reinforce themselves, as pessimism or optimism spreads. This requires knowledge of business, accounting, and valuation principles.

REASONABLE PRICE PRINCIPLE

It is never worth the value investor's time or effort to forecast when tops and bottoms are reached. If price is a fraction of value, value investors buy, knowing that there is a chance that the price will fall lower. Over long periods of time the gap will narrow and often reverse.

PATSY PRINCIPLE

Patsies lose money in stock investment. Market timers and others with the inability to assess the underlying value of businesses should not even participate in the art of stock selection and investment. Those so afflicted are like the patsy in poker, the person unaware that his funds will shortly be held by someone else. Poker and stock-picking are tricky enterprises, not for the overconfident.

CIRCLE OF COMPETENCE PRINCIPLE

Value investors make hardheaded assessments of their competencies. If they doubt their skill in stock selection, they steer clear. Value investors know their limits, thickly drawing the boundaries of their circle of competence. They avoid investment prospects beyond those boundaries as well as anything even close to the boundaries. This rules out broad segments of industry, enhancing prospects and economizing on time and resources devoted to studying businesses. Those who cannot even identify a circle of competence should avoid stock picking altogether.

For those who feel a need to allocate a portion of their wealth to stocks, choose vehicles other than individual stocks, such as mutual funds, index funds, or do so through a diversified retirement account. However, these operate as subparts of the broader market, and therefore can be over- or underpriced. This means applying the same ten principles of disciplined investing, but perhaps less rigorously so.

MOAT PRINCIPLE

Market gyrations, price-value discrepancies, and risks of overconfidence warrant exercising extraordinary caution in selecting an investment. In focusing on the business, value investors ascertain whether the business itself is substantially insulated from adversity. Value investors avoid businesses threatened by product market downturns, recessions, competitive onslaughts, and technology shifts. The business itself must be fortified by a moat, a defensive barrier to these ill effects such as arise from brand-name ubiquity, staple products, market strength, and adequate research and development resources. Franchise value is exhibited by high, sustainable returns on equity.

MARGIN OF SAFETY PRINCIPLE

Value investors worry that they might be wrong when complying with these first five principles. So they add a belt in addition to these suspenders. Drawing on the point that prices are different than values, value investors insist on as large a favorable margin of difference between them as possible. Doing so produces a margin of safety against judgment error. While none of these 10 principles should be ignored, this is the most fundamental and universal. Obeying this one promotes obedience to the others as well.

IN-LAW PRINCIPLE

The headline-grabbing accounting scandals of the early 2000s underscore the age-old importance of trust in investing. Value investors invest only in the stock of companies known to be run by faithful stewards of investor capital. They seek proven track records of good judgment and fair treatment. History is not always reliable, but any hints of malfeasance in a manager's record are enough to disqualify his employer. Value investors imagine managers of companies they are considering as prospective in-laws. If they would not want their child to marry a company's top manager, they don't invest money in that company.

ELITISM PRINCIPLE

Few stocks or other investments live up to these principles rigorously applied. Value investors treat companies as applicants to an exclusive club they run and wish to keep exclusive. It is far safer to make the error of omission than to make the error of inclusion. Those invited to join a value investor's portfolio after applying this elitist exclusionary policy can be invited often, more of their stock bought as circumstances warrant. It is far more important to diversify across asset classes—having a savings account, some bonds, real property, and stocks—than it is to diversify across stocks.

OWNER PRINCIPLE

The cumulative effect of these principles is a characterization of the value investor's role in corporate investing as the owner of not just stock, but a business. Hence the principles of business analyst, moat, margin of safety, and son-in-law. It requires appreciating stock selections in the same way the owner of a small business treats decisions concerning his store, farm, or firm. It requires a long-term view and means avoiding the rapid-fire share turnover characteristic of so many shortsighted market traders. That's what value investing is.

INDEX